RELIGION BY REGION

Religion and Public Life
In the Mountain West

RELIGION BY REGION

Religion by Region Series
Co-published with the Leonard E. Greenberg Center for the
Study of Religion in Public Life at Trinity College
Mark Silk and Andrew Walsh, Series Editors

The United States is a nation of many distinct regions. But until now, no literature has looked at these regional differences in terms of religion. The Religion by Region Series describes, both quantitatively and qualitatively, the religious character of contemporary America, region by region. Each of the eight regional volumes includes overviews and demographic information to allow comparisons between regions. But at the same time, each volume strives to show what makes its region unique. A concluding volume looks at what these regional variations mean for American religion as a whole.

Religion and Public Life
In the Mountain West:
Sacred Landscapes
in Transition

Edited by

Jan Shipps

and

Mark Silk

Published in cooperation with the Leonard E. Greenberg
Center for the Study of Religion in Public Life at
Trinity College, Hartford, Connecticut

ALTAMIRA
PRESS

A Division of
ROWMAN & LITTLEFIELD PUBLISHERS, INC.
Walnut Creek • Lanham • New York • Toronto • Oxford

Published in cooperation with the Leonard E. Greenberg Center for the Study of Religion in Public Life at Trinity College, Hartford, Connecticut

ALTAMIRA PRESS
A division of Rowman & Littlefield Publishers, Inc.
1630 North Main Street, #367
Walnut Creek, CA 94596
www.altamirapress.com

Rowman & Littlefield Publishers, Inc.
A wholly owned subsidiary of The Rowman & Littlefield Publishing Group, Inc.
4501 Forbes Boulevard, Suite 200
Lanham, MD 20706

PO Box 317
Oxford
OX2 9RU, UK

Copyright © 2004 by AltaMira Press

British Library Cataloguing in Publication Information Available

Library of Congress Cataloging-in-Publication Data Available

ISBN 0-7591-0626-6 (cloth: alk. paper)
ISBN 0-7591-0627-4 (pbk.: alk. paper)

Printed in the United States of America

♾™ The paper used in this publication meets the minimum requirements of American National Standard for Information Sciences—Permanence of Paper for Printed Library Materials, ANSI/NISO Z39.48–1992.

Dedication

This book is dedicated to the memory of
DEAN L. MAY
1938–2003
His life and work were an inspiration

Contents

Preface

Geographical diversity is the hallmark of religion in the United States. There are Catholic zones and evangelical Bible Belts, a Lutheran domain and a Mormon fastness, metropolitan concentrations of Jews and Muslims, and (in a different dimension) parts of the country where religious affiliation of whatever kind is very high and parts where it is far below the norm. This religious heterogeneity is inextricably linked to the character of American places. From Boston to Birmingham, from Salt Lake City to Santa Barbara, even the casual observer perceives public cultures that are intimately connected to the religious identities and habits of the local population.

Yet when the story of religion in American public life gets told, the country's variegated religious landscape tends to be reduced to a series of monochrome portraits of the spiritual state of the union, of piety along the Potomac, of great events or swings of mood that raise or lower the collective religious temperature. Whatever the virtues of compiling such a unified national narrative—and I believe they are considerable—it obscures a great deal. As the famous red-and-blue map of the 2000 presidential vote makes clear, region has not ceased to matter in national politics. Indeed, in this era of increasing federalism, regions are, state by state, charting ever more distinctive courses.

To understand where each region is headed and why, it is critical to recognize the place of religion in it.

Religion by Region, a project of the Leonard E. Greenberg Center for the Study of Religion in Public Life at Trinity College in Hartford, represents the first comprehensive effort to show how religion shapes, and is being shaped by, regional culture in America. The project has been designed to produce edited volumes (of which this is the second) on each of eight regions of the country. A ninth volume will sum up the results in order to draw larger conclusions about the way religion and region combine to affect civic culture and public policy in the United States as a whole.

The purpose of the project is not to decompose a national storyline into eight separate narratives. Rather, it is to bring regional realities to bear, in a systematic way, on how American culture is understood at the beginning of the twenty-first century. In line with the Greenberg Center's commitment to enhance public understanding of religion, these volumes are intended for a general audience, with a particular eye towards helping working journalists make better sense of the part religion plays in the public life—local, statewide, regional, and national—that they cover. At the same time, I am persuaded that the accounts and analyses provided in these volumes will make a significant contribution to the academic study of religion in contemporary America.

The project's division of the country into regions will be generally familiar, with the exception of what we are calling the Southern Crossroads—a region roughly equivalent to what American historians know as the Old Southwest, comprising Louisiana, Texas, Arkansas, Oklahoma, and Missouri. Since we are committed to covering every state in the Union (though not the territories—e.g., Puerto Rico), Hawaii has been included in a Pacific region with California and Nevada, and Alaska in the Pacific Northwest.

Cultural geographers may be surprised to discover a few states out of their customary places. Idaho, which is usually considered part of the Pacific Northwest, has been assigned to the Mountain West. In our view, the fact that the bulk of Idaho's population lives in the heavily Mormon southern part of the state links it more closely to Utah than to Oregon and Washington. To be sure, we might have chosen to parcel out certain states between regions, assigning northern Idaho and western Montana to the Pacific Northwest or, to take another example, creating a Catholic band running from southern Louisiana through south Texas and across the lower tiers of New Mexico and Arizona on into southern California. The purpose of the project, however, is not to map the country religiously but to explore the ways that politics, public policies, and civil society relate—or fail to relate—to the religion that is on the ground. States have had to be kept intact because when American laws are not made in Washington, D.C. they are made in statehouses. To understand what is decided in Baton Rouge, Louisiana's Catholic south and evangelical north must be seen as engaged in a single undertaking.

That is not to say that the details of American religious demography are unimportant to our purpose. That demography has undergone notable shifts in recent years, and these have affected public life in any number of ways. To reckon with them, it has been essential to assemble the best data available on the religious identities of Americans and how they correlate with voting patterns and views on public issues. As students of American religion know, however, this is far from an easy task. The U.S. Census is prohibited by law from asking questions about religion, and membership reports provided by religious bodies to non-governmental researchers—when they are provided at all—vary greatly in accuracy. Most public opinion polling does not enable us to draw precise correlations between respondents' views on issues and their religious identity and behavior.

In order to secure the best possible empirical grounding, the project has assembled a range of data from three sources, which are described in detail in the Appendix. These have supplied us with, among other things, information from religious bodies on their membership; from individuals on their religious identities; and from voters in specific religious categories on their political preferences and opinions. (For purposes of clarity, people are described as "adherents" or "members" only when reported as such by a religious institution. Otherwise, they are "identifiers.") Putting this information together with 2000 census and other survey data, the project has been able to create both the best available picture of religion in America today and the most comprehensive account of its political significance.

Religion by Region does not argue that religion plays the same kind of role in each region of the country; nor does it mean to advance the proposition that religion is the master key that unlocks all the secrets of American public life. As the tables of contents of the individual volumes make clear, each region has its distinctive religious layout, based not only on the numerical strength of particular religious bodies but also on how those bodies, or groups of them, function on the public stage. In some regions, religion serves as a shaping force; in others it is a subtler conditioning agent. Our objective is simply to show what the picture looks like from place to place and to provide consistent data and a framework of discussion sufficient to enable useful contrasts and comparisons to be drawn.

A project of such scope and ambition does not come cheap. We are deeply indebted to the Lilly Endowment for making it possible.

Mark Silk
Hartford, Connecticut
January 2004

Introduction

Religion in the Mountain West: Geography as Destiny

Jan Shipps

When automobile excursions to distant places within the nation became the vacation of choice in the years following World War II, tours of the Mountain West became so popular that *National Geographic* designated the region one of its "Vacationlands." Extolling the marvels of national parks, as well as the peculiar cultures of such enigmatic places as Sante Fe, Taos, and Salt Lake City, the nation's esteemed standard of worthy places of geographic interest published pull-out maps and stunning color photographs of scenic natural wonders that underscored and gave credence to the region's tourist booster claims. Beginning geography texts (often with some variation of *Lands and Peoples* in the title) and pulp fiction magnified the *Geographic's* presentation of the region. Hollywood films populated the area with western stereotypes, adding to a sense of unreality that made Montana, Wyoming, Colorado, Idaho, Utah, Arizona, and New Mexico seem like mythic places.

High plains, Southwestern deserts, and most especially towering mountain ranges do make this region a veritable scenic wonder. Miners, ranchers, farmers, cowboys, Indians, and even good guys in white hats and bad guys in black ones can be found among its inhabitants. But these states are much more than tourist destinations populated by people living quasi-isolated lives in romantic settings. In fact, only 19 percent of the 16,174,038 people who call this region home live on the range, in the foothills, in mountain villages, or on farms way out on the high plains. All the rest live in towns, suburbs, and cities where conventional patterns of American life are more the rule than the exception.

Because the region is integrated into the United States with extensions of the nation's political and social institutions in place and functioning, life in the Mountain West is American to the core. Indeed, in some instances it is super-American. But for a variety of reasons, this land is also distinctive and atypical. While four-fifths of the region's population lives in areas the U.S. Census denominates as urban, the population density in the region is only slightly more than 22 people per square mile, compared with 54 people per square mile in Washington and Oregon (the continental dimension of the Pacific Northwest) and 80 people per square mile in the nation as a whole. What emerges from this comparison is a picture of a land sweeping in its uninhabited expanse.

Throughout the region, open vistas lead the eye outward and, in much of the area, upward to the splendid panorama of mountains reaching skyward. Even though an overwhelming proportion of the population resides in towns, suburbs, and cities, in the Mountain West the closed-in character of urban life is missing because the spacious natural universe seems so near at hand.

How long this low level of population density is likely to last is questionable. Only in Wyoming and Montana was the rate of population increase between 1990 and 2000 less—in Montana only slightly less—than the national average. In the same decade, Arizona's population grew three times as fast as the rest of the nation, and the rates of increase in Colorado, Utah, and Idaho were more than twice as great as the national average. Taken together, these growth rates mean that the Mountain West is the fastest growing region in the United States.[1]

These seven states have many geographic and demographic elements in common. They also share the perennial problem of a paucity of water and, in the past, had mutual interests in opposing the gold standard. The issue of tourism is also in the public sphere, and the citizens of the region have worked across state lines to make possible a positive regional tourist experience. In addition, in all these states, the federal government owns huge portions of land. These issues have operated to make legislators from the Mountain West region colleagues willing to work across party lines, sometimes cooperating with legislators from other western states (California, Nevada, Oregon, and Washington) so effectively that they are collectively known as the "Sagebrush Rebellion."

Despite shared characteristics and common problems, however, these seven states do not fit together as a provincial unit. With dramatically dissimilar settlement histories, these states actually form three sub-regions. Each sub-region reflects the different manner in which European-American culture made its way into the Mountain area.

In New Mexico's Rio Grande valley, for example, Spanish Mission Catholicism brought European culture in 1598, when the first Franciscan priests came to stay in the land that would become the territory.[2] The Spanish government established a permanent provincial capital in Sante Fe in 1610, and Catholic priests soon followed to establish missions in the surrounding area.

A few American fur-traders preceded the Mormons into the Great Basin, out of which Utah and Idaho would be carved. But European-American culture actually arrived in the wagons that oxen belonging to the followers of Brigham Young dragged across the plains and mountains to the valley of the Great Salt Lake, as well as in the handcarts some of the Mormon immigrants pulled themselves. Finding a land covered with lush grass that sometimes reached as high as a horse's bridle, these "Latter-day Saints," as they called themselves, designated a spot for a temple of the Church of Jesus Christ of Latter-day Saints. Then they marked off the land that surrounded "Temple Square" in regular rectangular blocks, following a city plan with a temple at the center that had been laid out by Joseph Smith, the first Mormon prophet, when he sketched out the "Plat for the City of Zion." The Saints believed they were building the Kingdom of God in the "tops of the mountains," but the city that rapidly took shape borrowed much from city plans in the states east of the Mississippi River.

Religion was not the animating factor in the settlement of the third sub-region, Colorado, Wyoming, and Montana. Hunger for gold rather than God was what spurred the early settlements in the area that would become Denver and Boulder. Subsequent discoveries of gold and other precious metals in other parts of what would become Colorado, as well as in the land that would be divided into the states of Wyoming and Montana, led to the establishing of towns that would become instant cities (and often just as quickly be abandoned), whose governing structures and capitalist economic systems copied those of cities, towns, and counties in other parts of the nation. In this sub-region, religion followed the prospectors' discoveries and the coming of railroads to the territory, serving as it did in California and, eventually, in Oregon and Washington, as a civilizing force.

Unlike the organization of many volumes in this series in which the various chapters recount the stories of the several Protestant denominations, Catholicism, Orthodox Christianity, and Judaism, the chapters in this volume are organized to reflect the reality that this is not a cohesive region. They deal with the way religion came to the three sub-regions of the Mountain West and how it functioned as a cultural agent as well as an institution that served the needs of the settlers by creating structure that made community possible.

The chapters on the sub-regions are, however, neither histories of the sub-regions nor institutional histories of the several forms of religion that made their way across the mountains and into the land beyond them. Instead, Randi Jones Walker's chapter on Arizona and New Mexico, Kathleen Flake's chapter on Utah and Idaho, and Philip Deloria's chapter on Colorado, Montana, and Wyoming survey the current religious scene, paying careful attention to the ways in which religion makes itself known to the public, as well as how religion operates in the private lives of individuals and communities. Following their surveys of the contemporary situation, the authors move back in time to explain the religious background of the three regions.

Walker's chapter is built around the argument that rich religious strata lie beneath the surface in Arizona and New Mexico, and that, as a result, religion emerges into the public life of these Southwestern states in surprising ways. She takes into account the geographic diversity found in Arizona and New Mexico, as well as the growing diversity in their populations. In the process, she makes it clear that, both from the institutional perspective and from its public expression, the religious dimensions of the contemporary public scene are more complicated than is generally appreciated.

While Flake's account of religion in Utah and Idaho makes the obvious case that these states are the heart of Mormon country, she does not simply provide a standard account of Mormon history and Mormon domination of the culture. Instead, she explores the implications for a people and the culture they fashion when a persecuted minority group becomes the majority in a land where European-American culture had never before flourished. Drawing on her own deep understanding of Mormonism and Mormon culture, as well as her familiarity with the Mormon faith, its theology, and its worship practices, she puts contemporary public issues in context, making it possible to comprehend just how "a church with the soul of a nation" manages to function with reasonable success in a "nation with the soul of a church." In a concluding section that reveals how very shallow the claim of growing diversity truly is, Flake argues that the combination of a unique theology and a persistent cultural memory of persecution that modern Mormons hand down to the next generation of birthright Saints and across to the next generation of Latter-day Saint converts almost guarantees that tension between the Saints and other religious groups is likely to persevere far into the future.

Deloria's depiction of religion in Colorado, Wyoming, and Montana reveals how very different religion is in this sub-region. With no dominant institutionalized faith—although there are more Catholics than any other single denomination—religion in these states is, at some level, not unlike religion elsewhere in the nation. Here, as in the Pacific Northwest and indeed in many places in the United States, religion operates on a playing field populated with a substantial cohort of "Nones," of individuals with no connection to religious institutions. But in this sub-region of the Mountain West, that does not prevent the pursuit of victory on the part of conservative Protestant groups, a refusal to even try to keep score by other Protestant groups, and the presence of Catholics and Jews for whom religion is as much about identity as it is about anything else.

Complicating the situation, especially in Colorado, is the presence of an amorphous group of individuals who regard themselves as spiritual but not religious. Those who fit into this category—they would object to the very idea of belonging—follow a great variety of religious practices, often connected to the surrounding natural environment. Deloria's connection of religion and place is especially useful, and his treatment of how religion functions in the lives and cultures of Native Americans is especially strong.

Two chapters precede these three sub-regional chapters. As is the case in all the Religion by Region volumes, the first chapter deals in a forthright manner with the demography of the region. Written by the distinguished demographic historian of the American West, Walter Nugent, it puts down a foundation for the remaining chapters in the volume by arguing that this region is, in effect, an oasis culture. Using data from the U. S. Census as well as data sets that, on the one hand, summarize information about church adherence gathered from the judicatories of the churches and denominations in the nation and, on the other, summarize the outcome of surveys that reveal how people identify themselves religiously, Nugent provides an up-to-date picture of the Mountain West as well as a precise précis of how many adherents to different bodies there were in 2000 and where they were.

A second chapter that precedes the sub-regional chapters was written by Ferenc Morton Szasz, the author of a recent comprehensive history of religion in the modern American West.[3] His chapter, which deals with the entire mountain region, describes the key contribution made by the members of religious groups and their leaders as they created a social infrastructure of hospitals, schools, and other human service agencies. Szasz generally focuses on the activities of the historic mainline Protestant churches, but he recognizes that churches in the mainline are a function of history and geography.

In two sub-regions of the Mountain West, the very notion of Protestantism in any of its many guises as being mainline seems comprehensible only if the situation outside the region is taken into account. Although its strength appears to be waning, certainly in modern Arizona and perhaps in New Mexico, Roman Catholicism is still the mainline church. While Protestant bodies are growing, they remain on the cultural if not religious periphery. For all practical purposes, the Church of Jesus Christ of Latter-day Saints is the established church in Utah. Other faiths are tolerated or even encouraged, but the institutional form of Mormonism is *the* church. To a lesser, but nevertheless considerable degree, the same is true in Idaho. Szasz takes this historical reality into account and includes the founding of hospitals and schools by Catholic Sisters and Mormon brethren as part of the story of the activities of the religious mainline in the Mountain West.

Taken together, these five chapters and the book's concluding chapter, prepared by this editor, are designed to provide a useful depiction of the religious landscape in this marvelously beautiful but exceedingly culturally complicated region.

Endnotes

1. Nevada, a state that is sometimes regarded as part of the Mountain region, had the highest resident population increase in the U.S. between 1990 and 2000. It increased five times faster than the average rate of growth in the nation.

2. Searching for the fabled "Seven Cities of Cibola," Marcos de Niza had explored part of New Mexico in 1539. Coronado followed soon after, in 1540 or 1541.

3. Szasz, *Religion in the Modern American West* (Tucson: University of Arizona Press, 2000).

RELIGIOUS AFFILIATION IN THE MOUNTAIN WEST AND THE NATION

The charts on the following pages compare two measures of religious identification: self-identification by individuals responding to a survey and adherents claimed by religious institutions. The charts compare regional data for the Mountain West and national data for both measures. The sources of the data are described below.

On page 16
Adherents Claimed by Religious Groups

The Polis Center at Indiana University-Purdue University Indianapolis provided the Religion by Region Project with estimates of adherents claimed by religious groups in the Mountain West and the nation at large. These results are identified as the North American Religion Atlas (NARA). NARA combines 2000 Census data with the Glenmary Research Center's 2000 Religious Congregations and Membership Survey (RCMS). Polis Center demographers supplemented the RCMS reports with data from other sources to produce estimates for groups that did not report to Glenmary.

On page 17
Religious Self-Identification

Drawn from the American Religious Identification Survey (ARIS 2001), these charts contrast how Americans in the Mountain West and the nation at large describe their own religious identities. The ARIS study, conducted by Barry A. Kosmin, Egon Mayer, and Ariela Keysar at the Graduate Center of the City University of New York, includes the responses of 50,283 U.S. households gathered in a series of national, random-digit dialing, telephone surveys.

15

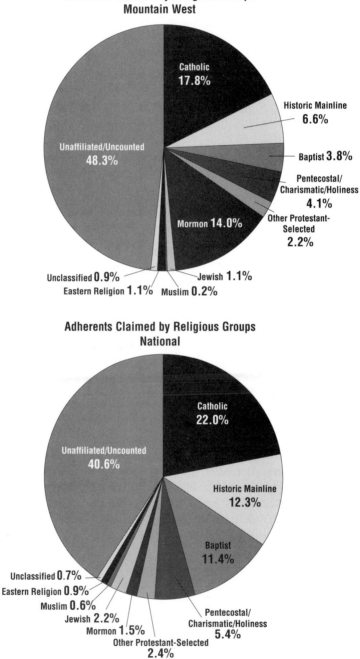

Adherents Claimed by Religious Groups
Mountain West

Catholic
17.8%

Historic Mainline
6.6%

Baptist 3.8%

Pentecostal/
Charismatic/Holiness
4.1%

Other Protestant-
Selected
2.2%

Unaffiliated/Uncounted
48.3%

Mormon 14.0%

Unclassified 0.9%
Eastern Religion 1.1%   Muslim 0.2%   Jewish 1.1%

Adherents Claimed by Religious Groups
National

Catholic
22.0%

Historic Mainline
12.3%

Baptist
11.4%

Unaffiliated/Uncounted
40.6%

Unclassified 0.7%
Eastern Religion 0.9%
Muslim 0.6%
Jewish 2.2%
Mormon 1.5%
Other Protestant-Selected
2.4%

Pentecostal/
Charismatic/Holiness
5.4%

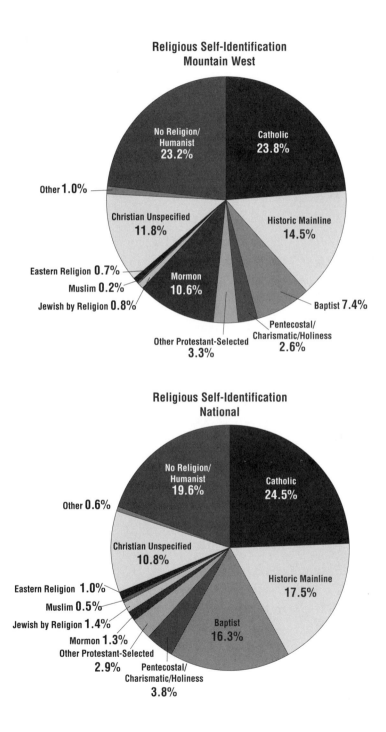

**Religious Self-Identification
Mountain West**

No Religion/
Humanist
23.2%

Catholic
23.8%

Other 1.0%

Christian Unspecified
11.8%

Historic Mainline
14.5%

Eastern Religion 0.7%

Muslim 0.2%

Mormon
10.6%

Jewish by Religion 0.8%

Baptist 7.4%

Pentecostal/
Charismatic/Holiness
2.6%

Other Protestant-Selected
3.3%

**Religious Self-Identification
National**

No Religion/
Humanist
19.6%

Catholic
24.5%

Other 0.6%

Christian Unspecified
10.8%

Historic Mainline
17.5%

Eastern Religion 1.0%

Muslim 0.5%

Jewish by Religion 1.4%

Baptist
16.3%

Mormon 1.3%

Other Protestant-Selected
2.9%

Pentecostal/
Charismatic/Holiness
3.8%

Chapter One

The Religious Demography of an Oasis Culture

Walter Nugent [1]

If any symbol captures the religious West, it's the symbol of a giant aquarium—God's aquarium. Throughout the wide spaces in God's western aquarium, there are schools of familiar (but easily startled) denominational species, there are slow-moving crustaceans, there are religious exotics from the depths and an occasional shark, there's the Mormon leviathan, and unchurched plankton are floating everywhere.[2]

Seven states—Arizona, Colorado, Idaho, Montana, New Mexico, Utah, and Wyoming—make up the Mountain West as that region is defined for the Religion by Region project.[3] This seven-state area is the United States' pre-eminent "oasis" region; in it there is a great deal of "empty" (i.e., unpopulated by people) space dotted with a few urban concentrations, often several hundred miles apart. Within the region, there are three sub-regions: Arizona and New Mexico in the South; Utah and Idaho in the Northwest; and Colorado, Wyoming and Montana in the Northeast. Although they share the region's oasis character as well as many geographical features, these sub-regions are noticeably different from one another. As this chapter demonstrates, however, their differences are marked more by their cultural and religious characteristics than by their demography.

This chapter is divided into five major parts:
- the general demographic shape of the Mountain West, 2000-2003
- the region's religious demography, 2000+
- the region's demographic history

- a brief historical survey of affiliations up to 2003, group-by-group, showing how religious affiliations have changed over time, and where they were in the first years of the twenty-first century.
- an appraisal of the connections between religious affiliation and political views on several current issues, 1992-2000.

These are followed by a brief conclusion. To avoid statistical confusion in this chapter, the names of counties will be written in *italics* and the names of cities will be written in Roman.

The General Demographic Shape of the Mountain Region: 2000-2003

The Mountain region has always been the least populated part of the country. Though it doubled in population between 1940 and 1970, and doubled again from 1970 to 2000, its share of the national population rose only from 3.1 percent to 5.7 percent.[4] Thus, only about one in 20 Americans (5 percent) now live in about one-fifth (20 percent) of the land area. In 2002 it housed 22.8 people per square mile, compared to 79.6 for the nation and, in comparison, 223.2 for New England.

Some of it, however, has grown as fast as anywhere in the country. Between 1940 and 1970, Arizona tripled, while Utah, Colorado, and New Mexico doubled. The same happened between 1970 and 2000 (when Idaho nearly doubled as well). Left behind were Montana and Wyoming, whose growth was well below the national average.[5] This schizoid pattern—fast in the south and center, slow in the north—resulted from the region's "oasis" character. Two big oases of population on either side of the Rocky Mountains, plus about 20 other officially designated metropolitan areas, exist amidst an enormous expanse of deserts, mountains, forests, and Great Plains. Along the western face, the Wasatch Front, is an 80-mile-long strip from about Ogden, Utah, south to Provo, Utah, centering on Salt Lake City, with Interstate 15 its artery. This includes *Weber, Davis, Salt Lake*, and *Utah* counties, where 1.76 million people in 2002 (76 percent of all Utahans) lived on 4.4 percent of the state's land area. Along the eastern face, the "Front Range," about 3.5 million people, centering on Denver, live in nine counties bisected by Interstate 25 from Fort Collins south to Colorado Springs: 77.2 percent of Coloradans on 12.8 percent of the land area.

West of the Utah oasis is the desert-like Great Basin, extending over 500 miles to Reno; few have ever lived there. East of Denver, stretching 500 miles into central Kansas, the Great Plains were once the final theater of homesteading, but people have been dribbling away since the 1930s, to the point where medical, financial, and even everyday retail services have vanished. And between Denver and Salt Lake City are another 500 miles—of Rocky Mountains. Their sprinkling of mining towns has disappeared or been transformed by tourism, skiing, and other recreation.

Within the Utah and Colorado strip oases, population has grown as fast as anywhere. Colorado Springs, a quiet little city of 37,000 in 1940, is now home to 361,000 (533,000 in *El Paso* county, in the 2000 census). Highlands Ranch, just south of Denver, ballooned from 10,181 in 1990 to 70,931 in 2000. In Utah, the most explosive county was *Washington*, around St. George in the southwestern corner; the county doubled in the 1990s to over 100,000. In the three northern states, the story was very different. Except for Boise, whose metro area rose 57 percent in the 1990s to about 465,000, few places grew fast or reached the 100,000 metro level (Coeur d'Alene, Idaho, Idaho Falls, and Missoula, Montana, were about there); others, like Pocatello, Idaho, Billings, Montana, Great Falls, Montana, Casper, Wyoming, and Cheyenne, Wyoming, lagged.

But Arizona and New Mexico, in the Sun Belt, surged. New Mexico rose 22.4 percent between 1990 and 2002, much of it in Albuquerque and the three smaller metro areas (Las Cruces, Santa Fe, and Farmington). Arizona led the entire region and reached 5.46 million by 2002. Its 48.9 percent growth rate was second in the nation only to Nevada's. By 2003, Phoenix' metro area (*Maricopa* and *Pinal* counties) held 3.5 million; Tucson (*Pima*) had 881,000; Prescott (*Yavapai*), 179,000; Yuma (*Yuma*), 167,000; and Flagstaff (*Coconino*), 120,000. Together, the six metro counties accounted in 2002 for 88.8 percent of Arizona's people.

The largest cities, of course, produced the most births and deaths. *Maricopa* led all 263 counties in both, and in numbers of in-migrants, both native-born and foreign-born. *Salt Lake* was second, and *Denver* third in births and deaths; but they led all others in out-migration. *Utah* county (Provo) had the highest birth rate in the region, 25.2 live births per 1,000 population per year, hardly dented by its very low death rate of 4.5, reflecting its young, pronatalist, Mormon, university-town population. Utah was unique in the region in having more outbound than inbound migrants; but with the nation's highest birth rate, it still grew. On the other hand, population *decrease* was very evident on the Great Plains, as young people moved away and the aging persisters produced few births and many deaths. Of the 70 counties in the region lying entirely in the Great Plains, about half had more deaths than births.

Trans-border migration, the bulk of it from Mexico, was highest (in rate as well as numbers) in Arizona, followed by Colorado, then Utah. Wyoming and Montana had the lowest rates of natural increase and of in-migration, reflecting their non-metropolitan, nearly stagnant populations.

The region's racial composition has changed little in recent years. The region is racially unlike any other; much more Hispanic and Indian, much less black and Asian. As history suggests, the region's highest proportions of Hispanic-origin people in 2001 were living in New Mexico (42 percent of its population), Arizona (25.3 percent), and Colorado (17.1 percent), all above the nation's 12.5 percent. In the other four states, Hispanics were scarce: Utah, 9.0 percent; Idaho, 7.9; Wyoming, 6.4; Montana, 2.0. Similarly, Native Americans were significantly more numerous in New Mexico (10 percent), and in Arizona and Montana (5 to 6 percent each), than the national 1 percent. In truth, Hispanic and Indian proportions were higher than those figures indicate, because the 2000 Census allowed people to identify as "other" or multi-racial. Nationally, 6.9 percent did so, but 21 percent in New Mexico and 15 percent in Arizona so identified. No state of the seven, however, came close to national percentages of African Americans or Asians.[6]

In size, the region's 16.2 million people in 2000 ranked sixth among the eight regions in this study. The region is the youngest, with the highest percentage of under-25s, near the bottom in the 25-to-64 cohort, and with the lowest 65-and-up population. Although the pre-eminent region of "wide open spaces," it ranked near the top in percentage of urban, indeed metropolitan, place of residence. It has the lowest percentage of blacks of any of the eight regions, the highest percentage of Native Americans, and is second (19.5 percent, behind only California) in percentage of Hispanics. This is not because of exceptional numbers of recent immigrants; it ranked only fifth in Mexicans and last in Puerto Ricans and Cubans. It was the leader in "Hispanics of other origins," in census terms: i.e., people living there since colonial times. These statistics are displayed in Table 1.1.

Boiling down the region's recent demographic changes to essentials, there are two salient features.

First, as the twenty-first century begins, its population lives in a small fraction of its land area, principally the two strip metropolises along the west and east faces of the Rockies, centering on Salt Lake City and Denver, as well as several sizeable cities all several hundred miles from each other. The largest were Phoenix, at 3.5 million; Tucson, at 900,000; Albuquerque, nearing 750,000; and Boise, close to 500,000. Then came 20 smaller metro areas ranging downward from about 265,000 in Fort Collins, Colorado, to 67,000 in Cheyenne, Wyoming.[7]

Second, totally unlike the mythical Wild West or the Old West, much of this population is recent, and population growth has been in metro areas, whose population explosions have more than made up for the stagnation and depopulation in mining areas and on the Great Plains.

Why this uneven distribution across so much real estate, and why the recent surge? An answer lies, as it always has in the West, in whether water has been available. But even nature has been rearranged by air-conditioning (making Phoenix possible) and, let it be said, by political clout. Thus these seven states divide demographically into a large land mass of mountains, deserts, and forests

**Table 1.1   Population Characteristics of the Mountain West
          Compared to the Nation**

		Mountain West	Nation
Population count		16,174,038	281,421,906
Land-base (square miles)		746,252	3,537,440
Population density (per square mile)		21.6	79.5
Percent living in a different state in 1995		30.2	19.5
Percent living in urban areas		81.3	79.0
Percent that are	Less than age 18	27.3	25.7
	18 – 44	44.1	39.8
	45 – 64	21.1	22.0
	65 and Over	11.1	12.4
Percent male		49.9	49.1
Percent over age 15 that are	Married	57.6	56.5
	Never married	26.2	27.0
	Divorced	10.7	9.7
	Widowed	5.3	6.6
	Married but separated	2.7	3.8
Percent that are	Caucasian	80.9	75.1
	Asian	1.6	3.6
	African American	2.3	12.3
	American Indian	3.6	0.8
	Hawaiian/Pacific Islander	0.1	0.1
	Other Race	8.5	5.5
	Multi-racial	2.6	2.4
	Non-Hispanic	80.5	87.5
	Hispanic	19.5	12.5
	Foreign born	8.8	11.0
Percent over age 25	Without a High School degree	15.9	19.6
	With at least a Bachelor's degree	26.6	24.4
Percent employed in	Management/Professional	33.9	33.6
	Sales/Office	27.3	26.6
	Service	15.3	14.8
	Production/Transportation	11.4	14.6
	Construction/Maintenance	10.9	9.4
	Farming/Fishing/Forestry	0.9	0.7
Median Household Income		$39,444	$41,949
Percent living in poverty		12.3	12.3

that was never populated; a sizeable area (the Great Plains especially) that is stable or depopulating; and a small but spreading component that is metropolitan.

The Region's Religious Demography, 2000+

There are striking differences in religious adherence (or lack of it) among the region's three sub-regions—the southern (New Mexico and Arizona), the northwestern (Utah and Idaho), and the northeastern (Montana, Wyoming, and Colorado). And they all differ distinctly from the other regions of the country. The differences have a long history, sometimes the longest in American history.

First, New Mexico and southern Colorado have a strong Catholic concentration. Part of it derives from the area's proximity to the Mexican border, which has given nearly all border counties from Texas to California a Catholic coloration. It is also long-standing: Catholic settlement of the Rio Grande valley began in 1598 and has been continuous ever since. It has sometimes led to exotic variants, such as syncretisms with Native American religion. Strong evidence also exists of crypto-Jews since the colonial period. Recently, the traditional Catholic presence has been massaged by three migratory streams whose impacts have conflicted: new migrants from Mexico and Central America; mainline Anglo-American Catholics who have been part of the net migration into the Southwest (more to Arizona than to New Mexico, though both states have experienced it); and mainline, evangelical, or conservative Protestants, arriving since the 1950s as part of the Sunbelt phenomenon.

Second: the northwestern sub-region (Utah and Idaho), and the adjacent fringes of neighboring states, are home to the largest, purest concentration of a single religious group anywhere in the country: the Mormons in Utah and across state lines into Idaho, Wyoming, Colorado, Arizona, and Nevada. This predominance began with the first Mormon settlements in the late 1840s, spread across and beyond Utah with the migrations of the second generation of Mormons from the late 1860s, and has never stopped. Brigham Young's proclaimed dream of a "State of Deseret" that would extend from the California coast to the Rockies is showing signs today of coming to pass as the "Mormon culture region" retains its heartland in Utah and keeps moving outward.

Third: the Mountain region contains a large proportion of religiously non-affiliated people, nearly as strikingly as the Pacific Northwest, which leads the country. Outside of Utah and Idaho, the unaffiliated (Nones) decisively outnumber everyone else and are in an absolute majority. True, some of these unaffiliated may have emotional ties to traditional denominations, as they do elsewhere, but formal affiliation is less common in this region than in most, except in the Mormon sub-region. From an Olympian perspective, then, the Mountain region's religious demography at the opening of the twenty-first century consisted of unusually high proportions of Mormons, Catholics, and "Nones," though not in the same places.

In 2001, researchers at the City University of New York conducted the American Religious Identification Survey (ARIS) asking a sample of 50,000 people to identify themselves religiously. In reporting the results of this survey, the researchers made weighted estimates of the adult population, shown in Table 1.2 (see page 26).

The second column, listing the numbers of people in the Mountain West region in 2001 who identified themselves or failed to or refused to identify with a particular denominational group, shows Hispanic Catholics to be the largest group, slightly more numerous than white non-Hispanic Catholics, with Mormons closely behind, and Baptists fourth. But those who said they were affiliated with no religious group outnumbered all three of these groups. The fourth column confirms this distribution: as a percentage of all those surveyed in the region, the no religion/no answer groups made up 23.2 percent, or nearly a quarter of the total. Next came Hispanic Catholics with 11.7 percent, then white non-Hispanic Catholics, 11.1 percent; Mormons, 10.6 percent; Baptists, 7.8 percent; and "other" (non-defined) white Protestants, 7.1 percent. Aside from two mainline denominations, the Lutherans and the Methodists with just over 4 percent each, all other groups were at 2 percent—one person in 50—or less. (It should be noted that if all Catholics—Hispanic, Anglo, and minority [black, Vietnamese, Filipino, and others] are lumped together, the Catholic population is larger than the "Nones.")

The third column shows how religious adherence in the region varies from the rest of the country. Recall that the population of the region is 5.7 percent of U.S. population at the 2000 census.

The ARIS survey's respondents from the region resulted in an estimate of the population of the region as 5.8 percent of the nation's population. Thus, the groups in column three that significantly exceed 5.8 percent are "over-represented" in the Mountain West region, and those significantly under that number are under-represented. (Comparisons with other regions, especially parts of the South, would be a lot sharper.)

"Over-represented" are Hispanic Catholics, Mormons, and the unaffiliated (and less prominently, Episcopalians, evangelical-fundamentalists, and Hispanic Protestants). "Underrepresented" are white non-Hispanic Catholics; Methodists, Christians (United Church of Christ), Quakers, Baptists, Pentecostals, Mennonites and other Anabaptists, Jews, Muslims, and very decidedly black non-Hispanic Protestants.

The pie charts ahead of this chapter of "adherents as percent of all adherents" for the nation and the region, based on data from the North American

Table 1.2   Estimated Numbers of Religious Self-Identifiers in the Mountain West and the United States in 2001 (ARIS)

Group	Religious Self-Identifiers in the U.S. nationally	Self-Identifiers in Mountain Region	% in MW of group's Self-Identifiers	Group as % of all MW adherents
Total numbers	207,982,828	11,961,183	5.8	100.0
Catholic				
White non-Hispanic	33,072,673	1,330,458	4.0	11.1
Hispanic	14,166,226	1,396,341	9.9	11.7
Black non-Hispanic	1,428,534	46	0.0	0.0
Other minority	2,205,939	118,012	5.3	1.0
Eastern Orthodox	635,510	9,516	1.5	0.1
Protestant, white, non-Hispanic				
Lutheran	9,203,966	503,198	5.5	4.2
Methodist	11,953,612	528,394	4.4	4.4
Presbyterian	5,070,469	255,285	5.0	2.1
Episcopalian	3,014,792	197,074	6.5	1.6
United Church of Christ	1,280,360	44,898	3.5	0.4
Disciples (Chr.)	467,000	26,738	5.7	0.2
Quaker	203,916	6,769	3.3	0.1
Baptist	24,481,124	937,580	3.8	7.8
Pentecostal	4,392,188	144,294	3.3	1.2
Evang./Fund.	2,737,684	182,280	6.7	1.5
Holiness	673,651	38,267	5.7	0.3
Mennonite/Breth	637,801	10,827	1.7	0.1
Reformed Trad.	330,999	3,239	1.0	0.0
Other	13,337,084	854,368	6.4	7.1
Minority Protestant				
Hispanics	5,689,440	430,861	7.6	3.6
Black non-Hispanic	16,342,213	176,184	1.1	1.5
Other	3,643,327	226,091	6.2	1.9
Mormon	2,697,308	1,271,637	47.1	10.6
Jehovah's Witness	1,331,172	62,708	4.7	0.5
Jewish	2,836,930	98,090	3.5	0.8
Muslim	1,103,813	23,638	2.1	0.2
Buddhist	1,082,332	57,916	5.4	0.5
All Other Groups	2,471,240	237,466	9.6	2.0
"No religion"	29,418,798	2,178,954	7.4	18.2
DK/No answer	11,307,050	596,639	5.3	5.0
Total	207,982,828	11,962,183	5.8	100.0

Religion Atlas (NARA) as reported by religious organizations, show parallel results.

The most salient differences between the region and the nation: Catholics (Hispanic and non) make up 37 percent of adherents nationally, but only 34.4 percent in the region. White Baptists, 14.3 percent of adherents nationally, are only 6.5 percent in the region's adherents; and black Protestants, 12.4 percent of adherents nationally, make up only 3.4 percent in the region (not surprising, in view of the overall racial distribution of the region). Certain Protestant groups exceeded national percentages: Holiness/Wesleyan/Pentecostals are 4.6 percent nationally but 5.7 percent in the region, and "other conservative Christians," 4.9 percent nationally, are 5.9 percent in the region. The outstanding difference is the Mormons; they are only 2.5 percent of the nation's adherents, but 27 percent of the region's adherents.

More than most regions, the Mountain West has radical differences within it with regard to religious preference. The chief reason is the geographical concentration of Mormons. When we separate the Mormon heartland from the rest of the region, the differences show up clearly in the size and rank-order of religious organizations. Table 1.3 (see page 28) separates the southern (Arizona and New Mexico) sub-region; the northwestern, strongly Mormon, sub-region (Utah and Idaho); and the northeastern sub-region (Montana, Wyoming, and Colorado).

NARA data show that in the southern and northeastern sub-regions, over half of the total population is not affiliated with a religious denomination or organization. In the Utah-Idaho sub-region, only a third are not affiliated. In Arizona-New Mexico, almost a quarter of the population are Catholic (23.8 percent) and in the Montana-Wyoming-Colorado sub-region, nearly two-fifths (38.4 percent) are Catholic; but in Utah-Idaho, fewer than one in 10 (9.7 percent) are Catholic. In the Utah-Idaho sub-region, just over half the population is Mormon, outnumbering even the unaffiliated (about a third), and over five times as numerous as the next group, Catholics. Mormons, on the other hand, constitute only 4.2 percent of the people of Arizona and New Mexico (despite the Mormon communities in the Arizona Strip north of the Grand Canyon), ranking fourth behind the unaffiliated, Catholics, and Baptists. The Mormon total in Montana-Wyoming-Colorado is only 3 percent, ranking seventh. As in the ARIS survey, the NARA data indicate that once the unaffiliated, Mormons, and Catholics are accounted for, no other group in any of the three sub-regions accounts for even 5 percent of its population, and most of them considerably less.

The Region's Demographic History

When people of European, Asian, and African heritage began entering the Mountain West over 400 years ago, they found other people already there. Well

Table 1.3   Adherents' and Unaffiliateds' percentage of total population in each of three sub-regions, and each group's rank in that sub-region, 2000 (NARA)

Group	AZ-NM rank	% of pop. in AZ-NM	ID-UT rank	% of pop., ID-UT	CO-MT-WY rank	% of pop., CO-MT-WY
1. Catholics	2	23.8	3	9.7	2	38.4
2. Orthodox	16	0.5	14-15	0.2	20	0.1
Mainline Protestant						
3. Lutheran	10-11	1.2	11	0.6	8-9	2.2
4. United Methodist	8	1.4	9-10	0.7	13-14	0.9
5. Presbyterian	14	0.7	12-13	0.4	12	1.1
6. Episcopalian	15	0.6	12-13	0.4	13-14	0.9
7. U.C.C.	17-19	0.2	20	0.0	15	0.5
8. Disciples	17-19	0.2	16-19	0.1	16-17	0.4
9. Other	12	1.1	7	1.5	3	4.0
Evangelical Protestant						
10. Baptist	3	4.5	8	1.3	6	3.4
11. Holiness etc	6	3.1	4	1.8	5	3.5
12. Pietist/Anab.	20	0.1	15	0.1	19	0.2
13. Conf/Reformed	13	0.8	9-10	0.7	10	2.1
14. Other	5	3.2	5	1.7	4	3.6
15. Africa-American	7	2.1	14-15	0.2	8-9	2.2
16. Mormon	4	4.2	1	50.9	7	3.0
17. Jewish	9	1.3	6	1.6	11	1.3
18. Muslim	17-19	0.2	16-19	0.1	18	0.3
19. Eastern	10-11	1.2	16-19	0.1	16-17	0.4
20. Unaffiliated	1	51.0	2	33.2	1	54.3

over half a million Native Americans populated the region, the majority of them in present Arizona and New Mexico; and their ancestors had lived there for well over 10,000 years. They varied greatly, from the nomads of the Great Plains to the hunters of the Great Basin to the Apache and Navaho herders of the Southwest to the Pueblo peoples in their several dozen city-states in the Rio Grande valley. The arrival of newcomers from Mexico, beginning in 1598, and from the United States, beginning in the early nineteenth century, resulted in conflict in much of the region and the decimation, sooner or later, of many Indians. It also resulted in accommodation, coexistence, and even syncretism in religion along the Rio Grande. Pueblos and reservations continue to be home to many Indians, and the region today retains the highest percentage of Native Americans in its population, at about 5 percent if those who identify themselves as dual-race are included.[8]

Europeans and Africans first appeared in 1598, when "the last conquistador," Juan de Oñate, led several hundred settlers, soldiers, and priests from central Mexico through "El Paso del Norte" and up the Rio Grande valley. The Spanish founded Santa Fe in 1609 and Albuquerque in 1706, and the area has been Hispanic and Indian ever since. Anglo-Americans started coming in some numbers in 1821 when Mexican independence from Spain opened the Santa Fe Trail to Missouri, adding Anglo culture (and in 1846 conquest) to the mix. The other half of the southern sub-region, Arizona, also had its ancient Indian cultures and, around 1700, missionaries from Mexico. Anglo arrival, however, came even later than in New Mexico, when precious-metal mining revved up after the Civil War and railroads subsequently opened the sub-region in both directions. Phoenix began in 1870 as a mining camp; now the largest city between Los Angeles and Houston, it is the only sizeable city between them that has no Spanish colonial origin.

Farther north, the Great Basin—our northwestern sub-region—saw its first non-Indian settlement when Brigham Young arrived with the first few hundred Mormons in 1847. The tribe increased rapidly, and in the 1860s and 1870s began spreading wherever water resources permitted. In the northeastern sub-region, the post-Indian phase began with the gold rush to the Denver area in 1859, followed by subsequent gold-seeking into Montana. The first transcontinental railroad crossed Wyoming and Utah in the late 1860s, sprinkling settlements along the tracks from Cheyenne to Ogden. The last pre-industrial population surge in the region came between about 1901 and 1920, when homesteaders poured into the far reaches of the Great Plains—eastern Montana, Wyoming, Colorado, and New Mexico—hoping for a final conquest of the prairies. Hopes were dashed in a great many cases, sometimes immediately, sometimes after the long agricultural depression of the 1920s and 1930s, and the post-1945 inexorable squeeze-out of family farms across the country.

The demographic history of the Mountain West region since 1920 is increasingly an urban, suburban, and finally a metropolitan story. Mining, farming, and ranching has continued, but have involved stable numbers and a declining percentage of the population. Migrants kept coming—a relatively small number of health-seekers and Dust-Bowl refugees before 1940, and an increasing number of Sun Belt-seekers after 1950. By 1970, the Great Plains were losing people and one-time mining towns in the Rockies were transforming themselves into resorts and recreation centers. The strip oases along the Wasatch Front and the Front Range had definitely taken shape. Isolated oases, led by Phoenix, were climbing well up the rank-order of the nation's metropolitan areas. The passenger trains that first brought large numbers of Easterners to and through the region, beginning in the late 1800s, seldom ran any more; over a 100 passenger trains passed through Ogden every day in 1920, but only two were running in 1985. By then, however, the interstate highway system made a trip of 500 miles a day nothing unusual, and along with commercial jet air travel made the oases accessible (and attractive to newcomers) as never before.

Since 1970, at least five major changes have marked the Mountain West population:

- large net gains have come from inter-regional migration from the East; from the Midwest, especially its snow belts; and from the coastal West, especially from southern California since the late 1980s to Idaho, Utah, and Arizona.
- these increases have come almost exclusively to metropolitan areas, principally Phoenix and Denver, but also smaller ones; the gains have not scattered evenly across the landscape.
- the age structure has changed, notably through the arrival of retirees in places like Phoenix; there the population has aged; in Utah, however, a high birth rate (highest of the 50 states) has kept the median age low.
- birth rates have slowed, even in Utah; the region kept pace with the nation in retreating from the high birth rates of the 1940s-1965 baby boom.
- in many ways the most important change of all, a change set in motion by the 1965 federal immigration law, led to more people in more places, and to different ethnic complexions; after that law took effect in 1968, opening up immigration based on family uni-fication and preferred occupations, people have come not only to the southern sub-region but also to Colorado and Utah from Mexico, central America, and parts of Asia (hence the rising pro-portions of Hispanic Catholics and of adherents to Eastern reli-gions).

A region that for over 100 years—300 years in New Mexico's case—was almost unpopulated, distant, and exotic became fully integrated into national pop-ulation patterns such as birth, death, and disease rates, metropolitanization, and immigration. In the latter two cases strongly so.

How Religious Affiliations Have Changed Over Time, and Where They Are Now

The Mountain West region was the scene of nearly the first European reli-gious establishments in the country, the Franciscan missions in New Mexico dat-ing from 1598, and the Jesuit missions in Arizona since about 1690. Preceding them, of course, were Pueblo, Tohono O'odham, and indeed paleo-Indian religions. Since 1847, the most successful Anglo-American group, the longest-lasting of the many religious and/or utopian products of mid-nineteenth-century America, the Mormons, have been a remarkable feature of the region's religious landscape. Recent decades have seen the influx of many people who have brought with them the contemporary spectrum from mainline liberal to evangelical conservative Protestant, Hispanic and non-Hispanic Catholic, and much else. This mélange may best be understood in parts, since (as already indicated) the three sub-regions vary so much from one another.

The southern sub-region, New Mexico and Arizona, contained a range of Indian religions. Some syncretized with Catholic Christianity following 1598, but others (Hopi and Zuni, for example) resisted and persisted. The Anglo-American occupation beginning in 1846 did not bring Anglo-Protestantism as notably as it did a more Romanized, ultramontane Catholicism exemplified by Archbishop Jean-Baptiste Lamy in Santa Fe, and a succession of Irish or Irish-American bishops in Tucson. A sprinkling of Jews arrived in the late nineteenth century, ranging in status and occupation from main-street merchants and small-town mayors to people like Wyatt Earp's wife, Sadie Marcus, and Big Mike Goldwater of Phoenix. The surge of population growth since the 1950s has meant more Mexican Catholics, more Anglo Catholics, more Anglo-Protestants (Baptists, evangelicals, and others), and more unaffiliated. This sub-region retains its historic tri-cultural religious face in the Rio Grande valley, but in Phoenix and the smaller metropolitan oases it manifests a cross-section of the Sunbelt in particular and American religious affiliation in general.

The northwestern sub-region—Utah and Idaho—is first, foremost, historically, and presently dominated by the Church of Jesus Christ of Latter-day Saints. Uniquely in the West, this one religious group, the Mormons, outnumber the unaffiliated. Catholics have been present in this sub-region since the late nineteenth century, but are a distant third in size, with mainline and conservative Protestant denominations well behind.

The northeastern sub-region—Colorado, Montana, and Wyoming—was originally the result of mining ventures: first gold, then copper. Along with the railroads (the Union Pacific in the late 1860s, followed in the 1880s-90s by the Northern Pacific and Great Northern), the mines attracted workers, many of whom were Irish Catholics, giving Montana in particular a strong Catholic coloration. For decades, Butte was a family-oriented, stable, Irish-Catholic place from the mine-owners to the most junior workers.[9] The gold-rushers of Colorado in 1859, 1893, and other times were not demonstrably religious-minded or affiliated, but the industrial miners of Butte and other mining towns certainly were.

Southern Colorado, a cultural extension of New Mexico, has tilted toward

Hispano Catholicism since colonial days. Because Montana and Wyoming have grown so slowly recently, well below the regional or national rates, historic affiliations (meaning a Catholic tinge, plus visible Lutheran strength in many Great Plains counties) have persisted more than in Colorado. The rapid expansion of the Denver metroplex from Fort Collins and Greeley south to Colorado Springs, resulting from in-migration as well as natural increase, has displayed a wide spectrum of denominational affiliations, not dominated by a single group or family.

Both the NARA and ARIS data sets have been aggregated into 20 denominational categories, of which "unaffiliated" is the twentieth. The following summaries use that 20-fold scheme and identify the areas in which respective denominations are strongest within the general population, where they are least numerous, and where their strengths or weaknesses have shifted historically.

Catholics

As Table 1.2 indicates, ARIS 2001 estimates 2,844,857 self-identified Catholics in the Mountain West (the total of the four racial categories of Catholics in the table), or 17.2 percent of its total of 16,536,000 at the 2000 census. The national percentage, 18.1 percent, is not greatly different. Within the region, they are the most numerous group, although markedly outnumbered in the Utah-Idaho sub-region by Mormons.

In the Arizona-New Mexico sub-region, Catholics are most numerous in *Maricopa*, as was true of most groups because of Phoenix's size, but are also disproportionately strong in the Tucson area, and in most of the heavily Hispanic and Indian counties, led by *Santa Cruz* on the border, where 87.3 percent of all adherents are Catholic.

Much the same is true in New Mexico, where they are strongest in the long-settled Rio Grande valley (34 percent of the population in *Bernallilo* [Albuquerque], 39 percent in *Santa Fe*, 60 percent in *Dona Ana* [Las Cruces]). They are weakest (though still 10 to 20 percent) in the Great Plains counties along the Texas border and in oilpatch *San Juan* (Farmington).

More than 50 percent of self-identifiers are Catholics in a majority of New Mexico counties, in southern Arizona and southern Colorado—historically so since Spanish colonial times—and in a few Montana counties, where descendants of Irish and German Catholic homesteaders and miners still lived. *Carbon* county in Utah, where Catholic miners came from the Balkans and Italy just before World War I, is proportionately the most heavily Catholic county in the state, but with only 13.8 percent, about 2,800 people. Otherwise the Wasatch Front oasis is less than 6 percent Catholic. Many counties in Utah and Idaho have no Catholic population at all, unique in the region.

In the Colorado-Wyoming-Montana sub-region, Catholic presence is occasionally strong (up to two-thirds or more) but spotty. The Denver-centered strip oasis varies by county from about 15 to 30 percent Catholic; Pueblo, historically blue-collar industrial, a little more (38.5 percent); *El Paso* (Colorado Springs), newly expansive with military and other retirees, a bit less (11.3 percent).[10] As will be seen, the proportions of identifiers in the major metropolitan areas of the region, always excepting the Utah-Idaho sub-region with its Mormon centricity, tends to approximate regional and even national, averages; big cities and suburbs attract everybody.

These patterns of 2000 and 2001 also reflect historic roots. In the 1906 census of religious bodies, the earliest such census, 83 percent of adherents and 53 percent of the total population of the copper-mining counties around Butte, Montana (*Silver Bow* and *Deer Lodge*), were Catholics, as were more than two-thirds of adherents in Missoula, Great Falls, Billings, and some Great Plains farming-ranching counties; all told, 73 percent of Montana's adherents were Catholics. In 1906 Colorado, the old-Hispano southern counties and mining or industrial counties such as *Pueblo* were strongly Catholic; most Great Plains counties, then undergoing settlement, were not; 48.5 percent of the state's adherents were Catholic, but only 18.5 percent of its 1900 population. Utah and Idaho, then as now, had few Catholics, 4.8 percent and 11.2 percent respectively; sparsely populated Wyoming had 11.1 percent. New Mexico was the banner Catholic state in the region, with 88.7 percent of adherents and 62.2 percent of total population.[11]

Leaping ahead a lifetime to the West of 1980—the point in time at which demographers define the West as having become truly metropolitcan—the distribution of Catholics reflected shifts in the economic and urban-rural composition of the seven states, as is seen in Table 1.4 (see page 34).

The continuing structural weakness of mining in Colorado and Montana reduced Catholic percentages (though absolute numbers rose); and the post-1940 explosions of metro areas—Phoenix, Tucson, Albuquerque, and smaller ones— diluted the Catholic predominance of the Arizona-New Mexico sub-region, but did not erase it. Mormons held their own in Utah and took a larger share of Idaho, thanks largely to their high birth rate.[12] In 1990 the strongest Catholic counties in the region (over 50 percent of adherents) still could be found in much of New Mexico, in southern Arizona, southern Colorado, and scattered across Montana. In most counties elsewhere in the region, always excepting the Utah-southern Idaho Mormon heartland, Catholics were either the largest single denomination with 25 percent to 50 percent of adherents, or, in the Mormon areas, in second place or sometimes third behind Baptists.[13]

Orthodox Christianity

With 0.1 percent of the region's adherents in 2001, the Orthodox Christian

Table 1.4	Percentage of Catholics in each state's population, 1906 and 1980						
	Arizona	Colorado	Idaho	Montana	N. Mexico	Utah	Wyoming
Catholics							
% of adherents 1906	66.2	48.5	24.2	73.1	88.7	4.8	42.9
% total population 1906	24.2	18.5	11.2	29.7	66.2	3.0	11.1
% of adherents 1980	45.2	38.1	14.9	40.3	56.7	5.4	30.0
% total population 1980	17.8	14.0	7.5	17.8	33.5	4.1	13.2

story is more quickly told. Metropolitan areas are home to most of them—18,031 in Phoenix, 7,041 in Tucson, another 7,000 or so in and around Albuquerque, perhaps 5,000 in the Denver metro area, 4,400 in Salt Lake and nearby, nearly 800 in Colorado Springs and in Boise, with some dozens elsewhere. Utah's *Carbon* county (around Price), where Cretan miners demanded and got their own Orthodox priest in 1915, still has 348 Orthodox identifiers, but most of the region's counties have none at all. Between 1906 and 1936, as mining declined and metro growth was yet to come, Greek Orthodox numbers in the region fell by almost half, but by 2001 as Orthodox adherents moved to the Sunbelt metropolises, the total had rebounded to about the 1906 level.[14]

Historic mainline Protestant denominations

Lutheran, Methodist, Presbyterian, Episcopalian, United Church of Christ, Disciples, Friends, Unitarian-Universalists, and some smaller bodies have been present in the Mountain West region for the past century or longer. Their spatial distribution reflects the homesteading settlements of the early twentieth century, which brought a cross-section of Protestants from the Midwest's farms to new farms on the Great Plains, and later, the post-1940 metropolitanizing trend that so magnified the Denver strip oasis and the southern sub-region's Sunbelt oases, again with a cross-section of migrants from the cooler parts of the country. The region has a few counties with unusual professional populations that have considerable numbers of adherents of historic Protestant mainline denominations. In *Los Alamos*, New Mexico, over 20 percent of the population is mainline Protestant in 2001, about three times the regional average. University towns sometimes approach that.

Separately, and even as a group, the mainline denominations have been quite small compared to Catholics, Mormons, and the unaffiliated. As Table 1.2 indicates, Methodists (4.4 percent) and Lutherans (4.2 percent) are most numerous, but collectively these denominations accounted for 13 percent of the region's religious identifiers (in the ARIS survey) and half of that, or less, of total adherent population (NARA figures). They are generally fewest in the Idaho-Utah subregion, where Mormons dominate. Currently the strongest pockets of Lutheran strength, 20 percent or more in some counties, are on Montana's Great Plains, where German Lutherans were original settlers. There are smaller concentrations in the Idaho panhandle and parts of Wyoming. Methodists appear in some hundreds in counties in northeastern Colorado along the South Platte River, in northern Idaho, some Great Plains counties in Montana and Wyoming, and in some thousands in the larger cities. Presbyterians comprise 13.5 percent of the population of *Treasure* county, Montana, and 7.3 percent of *Washington* county, Colorado, both on the Great Plains, but the actual numbers are small; identifiers concentrate in the larger cities. Episcopalians have virtually no rural enclaves and are even more urban in residence.

The United Church of Christ is well represented in Phoenix (nearly 8,000), followed by Denver and Boulder, Colorado Springs, Boise, Greeley, Billings, and Tucson, with 2,000 to 4,000 in each; but UCC identifiers are scarce in New Mexico and Utah. The Disciples of Christ's largest county is *Denver*, with 4,300, but they are fewer than 1 percent of identifiers. Disciples also appear in Phoenix, Tucson, Albuquerque, Boise, Laramie, Colorado Springs, and smaller places, though they are few in either rural or urban parts of Montana or Utah.

The remaining groups classified in this volume as "other mainline Protestant or liberal Christian" have similar distributions: present in some hundreds or low thousands in the largest cities of each state, especially in cities that have grown most rapidly since 1970, but very scarce in rural areas and smaller places.

Evangelical Protestants

White Baptists; Holiness/Wesleyan/Pentecostals; Pietists/Anabaptists; Confessional/Reformed, evangelical and Missouri Synod Lutherans; and "other conservative Christians" (including Seventh-day Adventists, Covenanters, Jehovah's Witnesses, and certain others) collectively comprise 18 percent of identifiers in the ARIS survey, with Baptists (not including African-American ones) nearly half of the total (7.8 percent). In the NARA figures for 2000, this distribution is confirmed: Baptists number over 100,000 in *Maricopa*, around 50,000 in Denver and its collar counties, and about 27,000 in Tucson, but there are only about 12,000 in the Salt Lake strip oasis; 7,000 in the Boise area; and 2,000 or fewer in four Montana counties. On the other hand, many Baptists were counted in and around Colorado Springs (*El Paso* county, 27,000), an area that is becoming a national center of conservative Protestantism.

In Farmington, New Mexico (*San Juan* county), swelled in recent years by oil and gas production, over 37 percent of all adherents are Baptists; and more than the expected number of Baptists are found in an area dating from the early twentieth century's first settlements, New Mexico's "Little Texas" counties along the Texas border, led by *Quay* and *Lea* counties (43 percent and 37 percent of total population) and in other counties whose leading cities are Hobbs, Tucumcari, Clovis, Artesia, and Carlsbad. As late as 1936, the region contained few Northern Baptists (most of them in Colorado) and very few Southern Baptists. But by 1980, 17 percent of New Mexico's adherents and 10 percent of its population belonged to the Southern Baptist Convention. Nowhere else in the region did Baptist figures approach those levels. (Culturally, it would make more sense if most of New Mexico's eastern border counties—"Little Texas"—were part of Texas, and if Texas' *El Paso* and adjacent *Hudspeth* counties were part of New Mexico.)

The other evangelical Protestant groups have sometimes spread themselves across much of the landscape and sometimes clustered in enclaves especially in the larger cities. The Holiness/Wesleyan/Pentecostal group claim almost 120,000 adherents in *Maricopa* (the Phoenix area), forming 3.8 percent of the population. About 30,000 (13 percent of identifiers) live around Colorado Springs; they also have about 20,000 in the Boise area (about 10 percent), about 6,000 in *Kootenai* (Coeur d'Alene in the Panhandle) and are represented in nearly every other county in Idaho. About 12,000 live in *Bernallilo* (Albuquerque) and 5,000 in *Dona Ana* (Las Cruces), 3,000 in *San Juan* (Farmington), and over 1,000 in several "Little Texas" counties, but are rare in *Los Alamos* and *Santa Fe*.

The Salt Lake strip oasis has over 10,000, and most counties in Utah have at least a few dozen, which most Protestant denominations could not claim. In Montana, about 8,000 live around Billings; nearly 3,500 around Great Falls and Missoula (each); and over 5,000 around Kalispell; several other counties claim well over 1,000. In Wyoming, approximately 3,000 live in both Casper and Cheyenne, and in two Plains counties one of five or six identifiers belongs to the group. Collectively, with about 7 million in the region, they rank fourth behind Baptists, Methodists, and Lutherans among Protestant groups.

The Anabaptist tradition had seldom been brought into the region as it was elsewhere by German immigrants, unlike the Lutheran incursions into Montana in homesteading days. An enclave of about 2,600 live in the Phoenix area, about 1,000 around Denver and Boise; and clumps of a few hundred each are scattered across Montana. Confessional/ Reformed, like some of the groups already mentioned, are numerous around Phoenix, Denver and its collar counties, Colorado Springs, Coeur d'Alene in Idaho, and scattered elsewhere.

Historically black Protestant denominations

Congregations of these denominations have never had great strength in the Mountain West region for the obvious reason that the region's percentage of black people lies well below the national average. Nonetheless, some adherents have become visible in recent years, particularly in the Sunbelt oases, while Denver has had a flourishing black community since post-Civil War times, and prior to 1940 had the only significant (3,000 in 1936) number of Black Baptists.[16] As of 2001, therefore, the southern sub-region includes over 78,000 black Protestants in the Phoenix area, over 25,000 around Tucson, 17,000 around Albuquerque, and 2,500-3,300 in three of the "Little Texas" counties. In the northern sub-region, 85,000 to 100,000 identifiers live in Denver or close by, plus nearly 40,000 around Colorado Springs. In the rest of the sub-region, however, black Protestants are scarce: perhaps 1,000 around Great Falls, 800 in Billings, and fewer in Cheyenne and Laramie. The Utah-Idaho sub-region has 13,000 in the Salt Lake area but virtually none elsewhere. Black migrants migrated westward out of Texas, Arkansas, Louisiana, and Oklahoma in droves beginning with the 1930s Dust Bowl and depression years, but most of them kept going on to California, just passing through the Southwest.

Mormons

Utah was the Mormon heartland from 1847 on, and it expanded in the second and third generations into Idaho and Utah's border counties in Nevada, Arizona, Wyoming, and to a lesser extent Colorado. Today the Mormons are the second-largest group in the Mountain West region (close behind the Catholics) and by far the largest in the Utah-Idaho sub-region. As indicated above, Brigham Young, who presided over the church from Salt Lake City for 30 years after the first migration, intended that a Mormon "State of Deseret" would encompass not only Utah but also present-day Nevada, southern California to the Pacific, three-fourths of Arizona, and large chunks of Colorado, Wyoming, and Idaho. The federal government thwarted the Saints, but much of Young's dream has come true except for southern California, and even there—in Orange County, for example—the Church of Jesus Christ of Latter-day Saints has a substantial presence.

By 1910, migration, propelled by high fertility, covered the Wasatch Front with Mormon settlements, with others sprinkled through southeastern Idaho, southwestern Wyoming, south-central Colorado (*Conejos* still has the highest proportion of Mormons to population in the state, at 27.4 percent), eastern Arizona, even into western Canada and northern Mexico. Since 1910, other migration streams have kept the area where Mormons are the dominant group from spreading, but Mormon numbers have continued to rise, and expansion has continued in other parts of the country and internationally.[17] The Mormon presence is so strong today in Utah and the southern half of Idaho that county figures are unnecessary. The banner Mormon county is *Utah* (Provo), where Mormons make up 97.1 percent of identifiers and 88.1 percent of the entire population as of 2000.

But elsewhere the presence is uneven. The Arizona-New Mexico sub-region contains several counties where Mormons are strong, led by *Graham* in eastern Arizona and *Catron* in western New Mexico, where 25 percent and 18 percent of adherents (respectively) are Mormon, while *Maricopa* (Phoenix) is home to 154,000 in 2000. But nowhere in the sub-region are they as concentratedly strong as in Utah and southern Idaho. Schismatic Mormon communities exist in the "Arizona Strip" between the Grand Canyon and the Utah line, but they are not numerous. The Utah-Idaho concentration, with weaker contiguous areas, continues a pattern evident in the early twentieth century.[18] Other contiguous areas where Mormons are the second-leading denomination include several counties in southwest Montana, just north of Idaho, and northwest Colorado.[19] In Colorado, several thousand Mormons live in Denver, each of the counties around it, Colorado Springs, and the old colony in *Conejos* county just east of the San Juan mountains. But many parts of Colorado have no Mormons at all (and, in truth, few people at all). Similarly, except for the parts adjacent to Idaho and Utah such as Evanston (*Uinta*), Wyoming, with 8,400 Mormons (43 percent of the population), Montana and Wyoming contain large areas without any Mormons.

Jews

The 2001 ARIS survey includes only those Jews who consider or report themselves to be religiously observant. They have been present in the region since its earliest European settlement, going back even to the crypto-Jews, the *conversos*, of Spanish colonial days in the Rio Grande valley. But in recent times, the more so as metro areas have expanded and small towns have stabilized or withered, one looks for Jewish congregations in the region in metropolitan areas. Reported figures—mostly in round numbers, suggesting they are estimates— include the Phoenix area (*Maricopa*) at 60,000; Tucson (*Pima*), 20,000; Denver-Boulder (*Adams, Arapahoe, Boulder, Denver, Jefferson*), about 65,000; Boise (*Ada* only, none in Boise city), only 800; about 850 spread across six cities in Montana; in New Mexico, 7,500 around Albuquerque (*Bernalillo*), 2,250 in *Los Alamos, Santa Fe*, and *Taos*; 600 around Las Cruces (*Dona Ana*), and 150 around Raton (*Colfax*) in the north. About 4,500 Jews are estimated to live in Utah, nearly all of them in Salt Lake City. In Wyoming, a few hundred are scattered among Laramie (site of the state university), Cheyenne, and Casper.

Muslims

Islamic adherents are a very recent addition to the Mountain West religious scene. The region lacked counterparts to even the few dozen Islamic families who homesteaded in North Dakota early in the twentieth century until some began arriving in the metro areas just recently. Today, Arizona includes an estimated 10,000 around Phoenix, 700 around Tucson, and over 800 in the northwest, close to Las Vegas. In New Mexico, about 1,800 are reported around Albuquerque, nearly 300 around Las Cruces, and scatterings in three other counties.[20] In the Utah-Idaho sub-region, about 3,500 live in *Salt Lake*, about 200 in the Boise area, and "163" (see footnote) around Logan (site of Utah State University) and also in Moscow (site of the University of Idaho). The Colorado-Montana-Wyoming sub-region has "163" in *Missoula* and *Gallatin* counties (homes of the University of Montana and Montana State University); nearly 300 around Billings; "263" in *Albany* county, Wyoming (University of Wyoming); about 14,000 in the Denver-Boulder-Fort Collins-Greeley strip, 600 around Colorado Springs, and 300 in *Pueblo*. The presence of Muslims in several counties with university towns (and almost identical numbers) suggests that many of them are students, while the large numbers in Phoenix and Denver also reflect resident Muslims' professional and service occupations.

Eastern (Asian) Religion

Strictly speaking, these are not new to the region, for Chinese have been present ever since the railroad-building days of the late nineteenth century. Filipinos, Japanese, and (since the late 1970s) Southeast Asians have strengthened the mix. Consequently, the region's large cities all have substantial numbers of Buddhists, Hindus, Sikhs, and other groups (treated collectively here). In the southern sub-region, Phoenix has about 28,000 identifiers, followed by Tucson (*Pima*) with nearly 11,000, Albuquerque (*Bernallilo*) with 10,000, *Santa Fe* and *Taos* with over 12,000 combined, Yuma with 2,500, Las Cruces with 1,400, and some hundreds scattered about.

The Utah-Idaho sub-region includes about 14,000 in the Salt-Lake-centered Wasatch strip, about 2,500 around Boise, and some scatterings (not many) elsewhere. In the northeastern sub-region, the university counties of *Missoula* (2,400) and *Gallatin* (1,100), plus Billings (900), account for virtually all identifiers in Montana and Wyoming. In Colorado, the immediate Denver area (*Denver*, *Adams*, *Arapahoe*, *Jefferson*) has about 38,500, with another 23,000 in *Boulder*. The counties encompassing Fort Collins and Greeley together have over 4,000, but Colorado Springs only about 1,100. *Saguache* county, high and isolated in the Rockies, has reported a very surprising (and somewhat suspect) 4,037 Eastern religion identifiers (and an anomalous 55.3 percent of adherents but 68.2 percent of total population).

"Unaffiliateds" or "None"

In this category are individuals who respond to surveys with "no affiliation," "no answer," or "don't know." Although the Pacific Northwest is considered to have the largest numbers and proportions of unaffiliated, the Mountain West—other than the Utah-Idaho sub-region, the Mormon heartland—is very close. The ARIS survey of 2001 showed Washington and Oregon as having 25 percent unaffiliated; the Mountain West, combining the "no religion" and DK/NA groups, had 23.2. The NARA results for 2000 show 33.2 percent unaffiliated in Utah-Idaho, but 51.0 percent in Arizona-New Mexico, and 54.3 percent in Colorado-Montana-Wyoming; the Mountain West unaffiliated may surpass the West Coast at least in proportions of population. Of the seven-state region's 263 counties, in no fewer than 128 (48.7 percent), at least half of the population claims itself to be unaffiliated.[21] These lay in northern and western Idaho, western and southern Montana, most of Arizona, Colorado, and Wyoming, parts of western New Mexico, and even two counties in southeastern Utah. Conversely, the most-churched parts of the region are a band of Great Plains counties across much of northern Montana, New Mexico's Rio Grande valley and Little Texas (the first Catholic, the second Baptist), and the Mormon heartland in most of Utah and southern Idaho.

Over the past century, some changes have taken place in degrees of affiliation. Using the 1906 U.S. census of religious bodies, the 1980 Glenmary figures, and the 2000 NARA figures, the proportion of unaffiliateds were as shown in Table 1.5.

Mormon Utah has become somewhat more affiliated, Catholic New Mexico and the other five states a little less so. (Wyoming's retreat from early infidelity may reflect the decline of its roisterous early railroad towns together with its small population otherwise.)

Do county-level figures tell us more? The highest numbers, but by no means the highest *proportions*, of unaffiliated live in metro areas. The largest, *Maricopa*, Phoenix's county, has 1.72 million unaffiliated, but that constitutes 56.0 percent of the population, right at the state average. *Denver* has 168,000, but a low 30.4 percent of its population, perhaps reflecting black and Hispanic residents; its suburban counties (*Adams, Arapahoe, Douglas*, and *Jefferson*) range between 60 and 71 percent. New Mexico's *Bernalillo* County (Albuquerque) has 37.0 percent unaffiliated which, like Phoenix, is almost exactly the state average. Even *Salt Lake* county has 270,000 unaffiliated, but the majority of this 30 percent of the county's population lives within the city limits of Salt Lake City.

According to the yearly statistical reports issued by the Church of Jesus Christ of Latter-day Saints, Salt Lake City's suburbs are much more heavily Mormon than the city itself. Despite the fact that Provo is home to two major institutions of higher learning (Brigham Young University and Utah Valley State College), *Utah* county, just south of *Salt Lake* county, has the lowest percentage

Table 1.5	"Unaffiliated" by state in 1906, 1980, 2000						
	Arizona	Colorado	Idaho	Montana	N. Mexico	Utah	Wyoming
1906	63.3	61.9	53.9	59.3	29.9	37.6	74.1
1980	60.5	63.4	49.9	55.7	40.9	24.8	55.9
2000	56.0	54.9	50.0	53.0	36.8	23.5	50.6

(9.2) of "Nones" in the entire state. Consequently, metropolitan residence is by no means clearly equated to lack of affiliation.

Counties with strong Indian populations, with a few exceptions, resemble state and regional averages. In Colorado, the mountain (and in some cases resort) counties such as *Pitkin, Eagle, Gilpin, Park,* and *Clear Creek* range from 65 percent to 94 percent unaffiliated, well above the state average, yet there are exceptions—a strongly churched mountain county, a lightly churched farm county—here and there. In Utah and Idaho, as one would expect, the rather few counties with higher unaffiliated rates are outside the Mormon area. Montana and Wyoming counties ranged widely in percent unaffiliated, but in some of the very sparsely populated ones there may simply not have been any churches to go to, and adherents would fatten the figures over the county line. Aside, as always, from the Mormon culture area, correlations of strong or weak affiliation rates with other characteristics are very risky; exceptions abound in both directions.

Connecting Religious Affiliation and Political Views

The political affiliations and opinions of religious groups in the Mountain West region and the nation have been surveyed in the ARIS project in 2001 for voter registration and party preference and, on three occasions during the 1990s, by researchers at the Bliss Institute at the University of Akron.

First, the ARIS results.[22] Nationally, 80 percent of those sampled are registered voters; regionally, 77 percent. Most groups in the region do not deviate more than a few percentage points from the same group's national figure. For example, white non-Hispanic Catholics are 86 percent registered both nationally and regionally; Mormons, 83 percent nationally and 80 percent regionally; unaffiliated ("no religion"), 71 percent in both; "don't knows" and "refused to answer," 68 percent nationally, 63 percent regionally. Hispanic Catholics deviate more than most: 70 percent registered in the nation, only 61 percent in the region. White mainline Protestants range nationally from 87 percent to 92 percent, and regionally from 85 percent to 92 percent; white evangelical Protestants from 78 percent to 87 percent nationally (except for Anabaptists, 68 percent), and 83 percent regionally. There are few surprises here.

The Bliss Institute surveys of the 1990s permit comparison of groups within the region to each other on eight hot-button issues and on partisanship. These data also permit comparison of regional and national survey results.[23]

Party affiliation

Because the numbers responding to this inquiry were small (under 100 for most groups), statements have to be cautious, but indications are that the highest Republican percentages are among "other Christians" (in this region, chiefly Mormons) at 65.7 percent and "high commitment mainline Protestants" at 61.3 percent, ranging downward to 23.4 percent for "seculars." Hispanic Christians are the strongest Democrats (56.8 percent), "other Christians" the least (16.7 percent). Most groups' party preferences do not differ greatly from region to nation except the "other Christians," more Republican (and Mormon) than elsewhere, and black Protestants, heavily Democratic but very scarce in this region.

Ideology (liberal/moderate/conservative)

The regional sample regard themselves about as liberal (30.5 percent, nation 30.9 percent), less often moderate (22.1 percent, nation 24.5 percent), and more often conservative (47.4 percent, nation 44.6 percent) than other Americans. High-commitment non-Hispanic Catholics are more liberal (39.6 percent) than their national counterparts (29.0 percent) and correspondingly less often conservative; a similar difference marks low-commitment Catholics. Hispanics in the region, however, are less often liberal (25.0 percent, nation 32.8 percent) and more often conservative (52.3 percent, nationally 32.5 percent). Again, "other Christians," surrogate here for Mormons, are more often conservative (53.9 percent, nationally 43.1 percent). Regional-national differences appeared among other groups, but not so sharply.

The issues

There is enough space here to note only the outstanding differences among groups and between regional and national positions.

On *abortion*, respondents could choose between pro-choice, "moderate," and pro-life. High-commitment Catholics are, as one would expect, pro-life (71.2 percent), but not quite as much as the region's high-commitment evangelicals (73.0 percent) or "other Christians" (71.6 percent). Compared to these groups, low-commitment Catholics are much less often pro-life (44.1 percent), and close to the national figure for their group (49.8 percent).

On *gay rights* (whether "homosexuals should have the same rights as other Americans"), regional views do not vary widely from the national sample except for one group, the "other Christians": 54.5 percent nationally, but only 39.2 percent in the region, favor gay rights; opposed are 28.1 percent nationally but 39.2 percent in the region, with the remainder taking "moderate" positions. The only other group with less than a majority in favor of gay rights is high-commitment evangelicals—32.6 percent in favor, in both the regional and national samples.

On whether "strict rules to protect *the environment* are necessary even if they cost jobs," every group nationally except black Protestants (43.0 percent) and high-commitment evangelicals (42.9 percent) agrees with the statement. But regionally, besides those two groups, fewer than half of the high-commitment mainline Protestants, high-commitment Catholics, Hispanics, or "other Christians" agree, though no group took a firm "anti-protection" position either.

As to whether "*minorities* need government assistance to obtain their rightful place in America"—which could be interpreted to mean affirmative action, or much else—the only groups in the region who strongly agree (1 or 2 on a scale of 5) are high-commitment non-Hispanic Catholics, and Hispanics. (Nationally, only 39.3 percent of the high-commitment Catholics strongly agree.) But low-commitment Catholics in the region are the group most strongly opposed (4 or 5 on the 5-point scale), at 59.3 percent; nationally, the same group are opposed by only 42.6 percent. The "other Christians" again vary from region (33.3 percent favoring, 49.0 percent opposing) to nation (41.2 percent favoring, 39.3 percent opposing).

On *welfare spending* (whether "the government should spend more to fight hunger and poverty even if it means higher taxes," only Hispanics (52.9 percent) are strongly in favor (two other groups are in favor but too few were sampled to yield reliable results).

Agreeing with the statement less often than the national sample are the region's high-commitment evangelicals (34.8 percent regionally, 43.9 percent nationally), high-commitment mainline Protestants (41.9 percent regionally, 48.1 percent nationally), low-commitment mainline Protestants (28.9 percent regionally, the lowest group, but 46.7 percent nationally), and low-commitment Catholics (36.2 percent regionally, 50.7 percent nationally). "Other Christians," on this issue, closely parallel the national sample.

On whether the country should have comprehensive *national health insurance*, the Mountain West sample does not deviate greatly, group by group, from the national sample, except that the regional "other Christians" (again heavily Mormon), compared to the same category nationally, less often favor such a program (39.2 percent regionally, 48.4 percent nationally) and more often oppose it (49.0 percent regionally, 38.3 percent nationally), with 12 or 13 percent both nationally and regionally taking "moderate" positions.

On *school vouchers*, an issue that was not on the 1992 and 1996 surveys but was included in 2000, the number of people sampled in the Mountain West was too small to permit valid conclusions. To generalize, perhaps too broadly, the positions of religiously affiliated (or secular) people in this region do not differ greatly from the American mainstream except that "other Christians,"—here but not elsewhere meaning essentially Mormons—take more conservative positions than usual.

Conclusion

In this vast region, so sporadically populated, the great majority of religious preferences are either Catholic (Anglo or Hispanic), Mormon, or unaffiliated, who most likely have all sorts of residual affiliations, preferences, and attitudes, which have yet to be explored systematically. The Mountain West is not as full of "Nones" as the Pacific coast, but has more than anywhere east of there.

Does "*Westluft macht frei?*" Perhaps, but another anonymous adage more surely applies: demography is destiny. Religious (or secular) affiliations depend first on rates of natural increase, the net balance of births and deaths, which account in some part for Hispanic Catholic and almost wholly for Mormon presence and increase; and second, on migration into the region. Migration began over 400 years ago and continues today from other regions and from other lands. The region's religious coloration will continue to be a function of these migrations and of the natural increase among both migrants and natives.

Endnotes

1. This chapter was originally to have been written by Professor Dean L. May of the University of Utah. He was felled by a heart attack in early May 2003. I have written this chapter with Dean May's scholarly and human excellence in mind. We regret his absence deeply.

2. D. Michael Quinn, "Religion in the American West," in William Cronon, George Miles, and Jay Gitlin, *Under an Open Sky: Rethinking America's Western Past* (New York: Norton, 1992), 164.

3. The Census Bureau also includes Nevada in this region, but in these volumes Nevada is grouped with California and Hawaii, for various reasons.

4. U.S. Census totals for the seven states, in millions, were 1.633 in 1900; 4.039 in 1940; 7.792 in 1970; and 16.092 in 2000.

5. U.S. Census figures (in thousands for the seven states, in millions for the U.S.A.), and growth factors calculated from them for the 30-year intervals from 1940 to 1970, and 1970 to 2000, are:

6. *World Almanac and Book of Facts for 2003* (New York: World Almanac Books, 2003), 365-89, 400; figures are for 2001. About 4 percent of the national population claimed Asian race; the Mountain West states ranged from 0.5 percent in Montana to 2.2 percent in Colorado. About 12.5 percent nationally identified as black; the region ranged from 0.3 percent in Montana to 3.8 percent in Colorado.

7. The Census Bureau estimated the populations of the metro areas as of July 1, 2002, as follows: Fort Collins, 265,000; Greeley, 205,000; Las Cruces, 179,000; Prescott, 179,000; Yuma, 167,000; Pueblo, 147,000; Santa Fe, 135,000; Billings, 132,000; Grand Junction, 121,000; Flagstaff, 120,000; Farmington, 120,000; Coeur d'Alene, 114,000; St. George, 99,000; Missoula, 98,000; Logan, 94,000; Idaho Falls, 85,000; Cheyenne, 83,000; Great Falls, 79,000; Pocatello, 76,000; Casper, 67,000. From census.gov, file /popest/data/counties/tables.

8. For more detailed treatments of the demographic history of the Mountain West region, see Walter Nugent, "The People of the West since 1890," in Gerald D. Nash and Richard W. Etulain, eds., *The Twentieth-Century West: Historical Interpretations* (Albuquerque: University of New Mexico Press, 1989), 35-70, for the 1890-1985 period, based on census figures, and Walter Nugent, *Into the West: The Story of Its People* (New York: Alfred A. Knopf, 1999), which looks at the entire West since the paleo-Indians.

9. The social history of Butte is well described in David M. Emmons, *The Butte Irish: Class and Ethnicity in an American Mining Town, 1875-1925* (Urbana:

University of Illinois Press, 1989).

10. NARA data base (Glenmary 2000), adherents by county, part 2.

11. U.S. Department of Commerce and Labor, Bureau of the Census, *Special Reports. Religious Bodies: 1906*. Part I, Summary and General Tables (Washington: Government Printing Office, 1910), 296 (Arizona Terr.), 300-01 (Colorado), 305 (Idaho), 334 (Montana), 338-39 (New Mexico Terr.), 364 (Utah), 373 (Wyoming).

12. The 1906 figures are calculated from the 1906 *Religious Bodies* census. The 1980 figures are from Bernard Quinn, *et al.*, *Churches and Church Membership in the United States 1980: An Enumeration by Region, State and County Based on Data Reported by 111 Church Bodies* (Atlanta: Glenmary Research Center, 1982), Table 3.

13. As indicated on maps C.10 to C.13 in Edwin Scott Gaustad and Philip L. Barlow, *New Historical Atlas of Religion in America* (New York: Oxford University Press, 2001).

State	1900	1940	1970	Growth factor 1940-70	2000	Growth factor 1970-2000
Arizona	123	499	1,771	3.55	5,307	3.00
Colorado	540	1,123	2,207	1.97	4,417	2.00
Idaho	162	525	713	1.36	1,321	1.85
Montana	243	559	694	1.24	904	1.30
New Mexico	195	532	1,016	1.91	1,829	1.80
Utah	277	550	1,059	1.93	2,270	2.14
Wyoming	93	251	332	1.32	494	1.49
Totals	1,633	4,039	7,792	1.93	16,092	2.07
U.S.A.	75.99	131.7	203.2	1.54	281.4	1.38

14. U.S. Department of Commerce, Bureau of the Census, *Religious Bodies: 1936* (vol. I: Summary and Detailed Tables; Washington: Government Printing Office, 1941), 388-89, reports the Greek Orthodox number (no Rumanians and only a few hundred Russians were tabulated) as 9,450 in 1906 and 5,505 in 1936. The ARIS figure for 2001 was 9,516.

15. NARA data base, adherents by county; *1936 Census of Religious Bodies*, 376-77; Quinn *et al.*, *Churches and Church Membership in the United States 1980*, tables 1 and 3; Gaustad and Barlow, *Atlas*, figs. C.10-C.12.

16. *Religious Bodies: 1936*, I:377, citing 1906, 1916, 1926, and 1936 figures.

17. Gaustad and Barlow, *Atlas*, chapter on Mormons, 296-308.

18. *Religious Bodies: 1936*, I:395, citing 1906, 1916, 1926, and 1936 figures.

19. Gaustad and Barlow, *Atlas*, figure C.12, "Regional Denominational Predominance 'Second Place': 1990."

20. Figures for each of seven counties—*Rio Arriba*, *Roosevelt*, and *Socorro*, N.M.; *Cache*, Utah; *Latah*, Idaho; and *Gallatin* and *Missoula*, Montana—are identical (163 people) in the NARA data base—which seems anomalous or suspect.

21. All had small populations and most were geographically rather isolated. Those counties with over 80 percent unaffiliated were *Camas*, ID., 98.2 percent; *Gilpin*, CO., 94.0, *Elbert*, CO., 90.7, *Park*, CO., 88.1, *Boise*, ID. 86.6 (not the city of Boise, which is in *Ada*); *Granite*, MO., 80.4. Glenmary 2000 figures on the NARA Web site: "Counties with Unaffiliated or Uncounted – Adherents as percent of total population > 50."

22. This ARIS survey sampled 34,294 people nationally, of whom 2,138 were in the Mountain West.

23. Done at the University of Akron and supported by the Pew Memorial Trust, the survey results are known as Bliss Institute data. The formal title is the National Surveys of Religion and Politics, 1992, 1996, 2000, collected at the University of Akron; John C. Green, Principal Investigator. The eight issues asked about in all three surveys were "partisanship; ideology [liberal, moderate, or conservative]; abortion [four choices]; gay rights; help for minorities; environmental protection; welfare spending; national health insurance." The 2000 survey also asked opinions on school vouchers. Denominational affiliations were compressed into 11 groups: (1) high commitment (at least weekly church attendance) Evangelical Protestants (non-black, non-Hispanic); (2) low commitment, same; (3) high commitment Mainline Protestants (non-black, non-Hispanic); (4) low commitment, same; (5) black Protestants; (6) high commitment Catholics (non-black, non-Hispanic); (7) low commitment, same; (8) Hispanic Christians; (9) "Other Christians (such as Latter-day Saints, Eastern Orthodox, black Catholics, etc.);" (10) non-Christians ("Jews and all others"); (11) "secular." As Mormons are such a large group in the Mountain West, it would have been more helpful if they had been placed in a category by themselves, but since Orthodox, black Catholics, and "etc." are few in the region, presumably group 9 means mostly Mormons in the figures for this region.

CHAPTER TWO

HOW RELIGION CREATED AN
INFRASTRUCTURE FOR THE MOUNTAIN WEST

Ferenc Morton Szasz

The dominant spiritual force in the Mountain West is the landscape that stretches from the low deserts of Arizona and New Mexico through the Colorado Rockies and the Utah Uintahs to the high plains of Montana. It contains some of the most spectacular scenery in the nation. This "force of nature" may explain why the region abounds in places deemed sacred to many religious traditions.

- For Native Americans, Taos Blue Lake and Zuni Salt Lake (both in New Mexico), Canon de Chelly (Arizona), and the Wyoming Medicine Wheel and Devil's Tower (Bear Lodge), are only a few of many Indian sacred sites.[1]
- For Roman Catholics, the modest shrine at Chimayo (founded in 1816), one of the world's few healing sites, is widely known as "the American Lourdes."
- For the Church of Jesus Christ of Latter-day Saints and its members (the Mormons), the entire Salt Lake Valley, with all its historic connections to the establishment of Zion in the West has a quasi-sacred character.
- Similarly, Sante Fe and Chaco Canyon in New Mexico; Sedona, Arizona; and Boulder, Colorado serve as magnets for spiritual seekers from around the globe.
- For Christians with institutional connections and those without such connections but with general Christian sensibilities, there is the 42-foot-high statue of Christ of the Rockies—larger than the far-better-known Christ of the Andes—that overlooks the historic Pass of the North (El Paso) between the United States and Mexico.

In short, the Mountain West abounds with places that community activities have made sacred to a number of religious traditions. In this region, the sacred overflows every conceivable denominational boundary.

As a glance at regional telephone books will show, virtually every major religious group is represented in this region of the United States. Still, the religious landscape of the Mountain West is considerably different from any other section of the country. A good place to start is with the architecture, for no area boasts as many striking religious buildings. Many of the Franciscan and Jesuit structures date from the seventeenth or eighteenth centuries, with styles that range from humble adobe mission churches to the towering San Xaveri del Bac, "the white dove of the desert," south of Tucson. The restored Old Cataldo Mission in Idaho and St. Ignatius Mission in Montana (both 1850s) reflect the strong Jesuit presence among the Native Americans in the North Country. The white clapboard ethnic churches of the Great Plains have equal appeal to artists, and the brooding adobe church in Ranchos de Taos, New Mexico, is said to be the most photographed/painted religious building in the country.[2]

Large Protestant Episcopal cathedrals still dominate many of regional city centers, especially in Laramie, Boise, and Denver. Also in Boise is the imposing First United Methodist Church, which—although it was never the seat of a bishop—is called the "Cathedral of the Rockies." While most of the early synagogues, with their prominent Near Eastern motifs, have fallen to the wrecker's ball, those in Boise, El Paso, and Denver still reflect this architectural heritage.

The most stunning religious architecture of the region belongs to the Latter-day Saints. In Utah, their towering white temples at Manti, St. George, and Logan instantly command the eye, and the famed Temple Square in downtown Salt Lake City ranks as one of the five most visited venues in the nation. For years, the Mormon temple in Salt Lake stood as the most impressive building, religious or secular, from Chicago to the Pacific Coast. The great dome-shaped Mormon Tabernacle, constructed in 1867 (home to the Mormon Tabernacle Choir), is located alongside on Temple Square. Adjacent to the historic buildings on its central campus—sometimes called the Mormon Vatican—the Church of Jesus Christ of Latter-day Saints has added a Conference Center with 21,000 seats with a clear view of the rostrum, making it the largest indoor theater-style auditorium in the world. The church also has other temples in the Mountain West, in Mesa and Snowflake, Arizona; Denver, Colorado; Boise and Idaho Falls, Idaho; Billings, Montana; Albuquerque, New Mexico; and American Fork, Monticello, Ogden, Provo, South Jordan, and Vernal, Utah. But none of these twentieth-century temples has the architectural distinction of those built in the nineteenth century.

The Mountain West reflects other unique religious themes as well. Generally speaking, the region has experienced minimal anti-Semitism. Jewish pioneers helped write the first constitution of Colorado and served as mayors, sheriffs, and governors in New Mexico, Idaho, and Arizona, well before they did so in Illinois and New York, states with much larger Jewish populations. Simon Bamberger, elected in 1916 as the first non-Mormon governor of Utah, was also Jewish. During the late-nineteenth century, German-Jewish merchants helped revolutionize the economy of the region, and turn-of-the-century Colfax Avenue in Denver, the center of regional Judaism, was once described as "the longest street in the world" because it extended "from Colorado to Jerusalem."[3]

Although there are a fair number of small religious colleges, the area contains only two large denominational universities: the University of Denver and Brigham Young University in Provo, Utah. In 1857, John Evans, the founder of Northwestern University (in Evanston, Illinois) who had been sent to Colorado as territorial governor, founded Denver Seminary as an institution of the Methodist Episcopal Church. When Iliff Theological Seminary was founded 35 years later as a ministerial training school for Methodist pastors for the West, it became a part of this institution, which was renamed the University of Denver. Iliff is the only United Methodist seminary in the Mountain West; the University of Denver continues to be affiliated with the United Methodist Church, but that connection is not close enough for it to be mentioned on the university's Web site.

Brigham Young University, on the other hand, is owned and operated by the Church of Jesus Christ of Latter-day Saints. Its Board of Trustees is made up of General Authorities of the church, and its students (who come from all over the globe) are primarily, but not exclusively, Mormon. Ricks College, a Mormon Stake Academy in Rexsburg, Idaho, which became a two-year college in 1915, has been transformed into a four-year institution and renamed Brigham Young University Idaho. (The students call this institution "The 'Y' of 'I'.")

Over the years, the various churches attempted to establish denominational colleges, but they seldom had sufficient funds and/or numbers to allow them to survive. An exception is Westminster College, founded as a Presbyterian preparatory school in Salt Lake City in 1875. In 1911, it became a junior college and moved to a new status as a four-year liberal arts college in 1949. Now funded by a Protestant consortium, it is an independent non-denominational institution that actually had to draw upon financial aid from the Latter-day Saints (LDS) Church during a recent economic crisis.

Thus, the great majority of students in this region are educated in large state universities rather than private, denominational schools. This makes the denominational campus minister a person of special importance in the Mountain West.

Most historians agree that the Mountain West contains no overriding institutional religious "mainstream" as (say) one might find in the largely evangelical

South or Catholic New England. Historically speaking, however, the region contained three distinct "sub mainstreams": the individualist, largely secular atmosphere of the predominantly male mining camps and railroad towns; the prevailing Spanish Catholicism of the Southwest; and the Mormon culture area in Utah and southern Idaho.

The secular individualism that characterized the mining and railroad towns has largely faded today, although one might, perhaps, find echoes of it in the non-conventional lifestyles and belief patterns associated with Sedona, Arizona, Santa Fe, and various mountain-based communal groups. Although still a social force to be reckoned with, the Spanish Catholic Church in the Southwest now shares its cultural influence with a wide variety of other faiths. But the Latter-day Saints' Kingdom of Zion continues to manifest a cultural hegemony that Brigham Young would easily recognize. In this area, as in virtually no other part of the nation, a person's identity depends largely on whether one is or is not a member of the dominant faith.

From the mid-nineteenth century to the present day, the major American denominations—European-based Roman Catholicism; the historic Protestant mainline (Baptists, Lutherans, Congregationalists, Methodists, Presbyterians, and Episcopalians); and Reform Judaism have largely functioned as "outsiders" in the Mormon corridor (Utah and Idaho) and the Southwest (Arizona and New Mexico). In nineteenth-century Colorado, Wyoming, and Montana, these religious groups—and indeed religion generally—initially seemed alien to the secularized culture. Charting the main ways by which these "outsiders" have interacted with this unique religio-cultural environment and created an institutional infrastructure for the region is the main business of this chapter.

The responses of the several church and denominational bodies fell largely into two broad, overlapping categories. From the mid-nineteenth century to c. 1920, the mainline groups essentially *created* the major institutions of the region—hundreds of churches and scores of schools, hospitals, and orphanages. By the middle of the twentieth century, local and state governments had largely taken over these educational, health, and welfare roles. Many of those not subsumed into the governmental sector were turned over to non-profit agencies, some still connected to religious institutions and some not. Consequently, the mainstream groups switched to providing a variety of religious programs. From the 1940s to the mid-1960s, the denominational programs marched together in relative harmony. But with the onset of the 1960s, the center began to collapse. Suddenly, the mainline faiths found themselves losing ground to a variety of forces: an individualistic "spirituality" that emphasized experience over historical group loyalty; a variety of New Religious Movements (NRMs); and, for the mainline Protestants, a powerful conservative evangelical upsurge that seemed to claim the term "Christian" as its own. Yet a thread of continuity runs through this century and a half of interaction. From the initial contact to the present day, the mainline groups have viewed their missions as providing for both the needs of their parishioners and for those of the community at large.

Building Institutions, c. 1850 to c. 1930

When the United States acquired the American Southwest after the Mexican-American War of 1846-48, Americans met a Spanish Catholicism that had been merged with the Native faith traditions for over a century and a half. In order to bring this syncretic regional Catholicism into the European mainstream, the Vatican designated French immigrant Jean Baptist Lamy as Vicar Apostolic of New Mexico; in 1852 Lamy invited the Sisters of Loretto at the Foot of the Cross to Sante Fe to establish a boarding school and a day school.[4] Within a few years, the Sisters had expanded their schools throughout what is now New Mexico to include Taos, Mora, Las Vegas, Bernalillo, Socorro, and Albuquerque. Their all-girls Loretto Academy in Las Cruces (1870-1944) emerged as the jewel of their parochial school crown. Both a boarding and a day school, the academy drew students from all over the Southwest and Mexico. It educated a number of non-Catholics as well.[5] In nearby Arizona, the Sisters of St. Joseph of Corondolet arrived in 1870 to establish the Tucson parochial school system, which similarly began to flourish. Simultaneously, the Brothers of the Christian Schools (Christian Brothers) established a school for boys in Santa Fe—now the College of Santa Fe. The wealthiest Southwestern families, however, continued to send their sons to the Jesuit-run St. Louis University for a more comprehensive education.

When the New Mexico public school system finally emerged in the early twentieth century, the far-flung Catholic schools in the northern part of the state simply became the public schools. As late as 1940, members of religious orders taught in some 30 regional public schools. This situation ended only in the early 1950s when Protestants in Dixon, New Mexico, sued—one nun was allegedly accused of teaching "Catholic physical education"—and the archbishop withdrew the sisters so as to avoid controversy.

When the Protestants arrived in modest numbers in the Southwest in the 1870s, they were appalled at the lack of educational opportunities. Consequently, Methodists, Congregationalists, Episcopalians, and (especially) Presbyterians began to establish their own parallel parochial school systems. Methodist educators Thomas and Emily Harwood led the effort to erect the denomination's boys' and girls' training schools in Tucson, Albuquerque, Farmington, and (later) in El Paso, Texas. The element of religious rivalry could hardly be missed. Said Thomas, "We have often said that the church that educates will surely win."[6]

No group responded to this challenge with more vigor than the Northern

Presbyterians. From the 1870s to the early twentieth century, the church established over 50 "plaza schools" in northern New Mexico and southern Colorado, as well as a short-lived College of the Southwest (1884-1901) in Del Norte, Colorado. Pioneer church educator Sheldon Jackson summed up the situation thus: "They won't come to hear preachers; send us a [female] teacher."[7] Consequently, hundreds of well-educated, mostly single young women taught for a year or two in the Presbyterian parochial schools of the Mountain West, and a few spent their entire careers in such service. The Presbyterians eventually phased out the parallel school system in the early twentieth century, when the public schools finally became effective. Only the Menaul School in Albuquerque remains today.

The Protestant response to Mormon Utah followed along the exact same lines. By the time non-Mormons—the Mormons called them Gentiles—arrived in Zion in the mid-1860s, the Saints had lived in the Great Basin for a generation. The editor of this volume, Jan Shipps, has argued that in their move from the Mississippi Valley to the Mountain West, the Mormons recapitulated the flight of the ancient Hebrews from Egypt and, by "re-enacting" the Exodus journey, essentially forged themselves into a peculiar people as described in 1 Peter 2:9: "a peculiar people, a holy nation, a royal priesthood."[8]

Although some Protestant clerics claimed that the Mormons had no schools before 1860, that is not exactly accurate. The Mormons chartered the University of Utah in 1850, but it took a few years to materialize, and when it did it was not a college but a high school. (The University of Utah is now the state's premier public university.) The Mormons established a variety of schools from 1849-1864, largely "fee schools," where local communities taxed themselves to pay for the buildings but left teachers' salaries and other expenses to be paid by the parents. Brigham Young always felt that parents should pay for the education of their children.

As in New Mexico, as soon as the Protestants arrived in Utah, they began to establish their own set of parochial schools. The Episcopalians opened theirs in 1867, the Methodists in 1870, the Presbyterians in 1875, and the Congregationalists in 1880. "I am confident that this is *the way* and the only way," said a Congregational cleric. In 1891, the Episcopal Bishop of Nevada and Utah termed the church schools "the cheapest and most efficient missionary agents we can employ in the [small Utah and Idaho] towns."[9]

Again, the middle-class Presbyterians led the charge as they forged the most comprehensive system of parochial schools: grade schools in each of the six main valleys of the state; various academies (high schools); and at the apex of their system, Westminster College in Salt Lake City. In 1890, about 67 percent of Utah's children were enrolled in Protestant mission schools, where virtually all the teachers were female. This parallel school system faded in the early twentieth century with the rise of effective Utah public schooling, and only Rowland Hall-St. Marks (Episcopal) and Mount Pleasant (Presbyterian) remain today. In essence, the mainstream Protestant parochial school system rose and fell in three generations.[10]

In retrospect, one can make three generalizations about this unique Protestant venture into the field of parochial education. First, initially at least, the potential for sectarian conflict remained fierce. Few held any doubts about the goals of these Protestant schools. Still, overt conflict in both New Mexico and Utah remained minimal. The reason for this lay primarily with the mainline decision to employ young women as teachers. These women teachers had access to Hispanic and Mormon home life in ways that men simply did not. The quotidian tasks of cooking, baking, cleaning, taking care of children, and simply gossiping allowed the women to learn about each other's cultures. Indeed, as the historians Mark Banker, Sarah Deutsch, and Randi Jones Walker have argued, these long-term missionaries often became some of the nation's first "multi-culturalists," as they slowly learned to walk in the shoes of their counterparts.[11] In turn, the "natives" eventually accepted the missionary women as one of theirs.

Second, the vast spaces of the Mountain West also helped to mitigate harsh sectarian conflict. Unlike (say) more compact South Boston, the towns in New Mexico and Utah were so isolated that they generally accepted all types of educational efforts. The historian Sidney Mead once suggested that space in America played the role that time played in the history of Europe.[12] It certainly seems to have done so here, for in spite of the presence of parallel Protestant, Catholic, and public school systems, until about 1930 many Utah and New Mexico children fell through the educational net.

Third, the Protestant parochial educational system never quite produced the results that their leaders had anticipated. Hispanic and Mormon youth drew readily on the educational opportunities, but they often bent them along their own trajectories. Here, of course, all conclusions must be somewhat speculative. In the Southwest today, the Catholic School system, albeit somewhat reduced in number, still performs a vital educational role. But the region also abounds with numerous Hispanic Baptists, Methodists, Congregationalists, and Presbyterians as well. Some are recent converts to a Pentecostal or evangelical faith, but a number of Hispanic Protestants trace their heritage back to an ancestor's attendance at the various mission schools of the late nineteenth and early twentieth centuries.

If the mainline parochial school systems in New Mexico helped forge a Hispanic Protestant sub stratum, the story in Utah is quite different. From 1870-1920, the Protestant population there rose only in direct proportion to non-Mormon immigration. This meant that, although the level of their activity varied widely, relatively few Mormons ever left the church. In fact, some have suggested that Protestant schooling simply provided the Mormons with skills by which they could better defend their own faith perspective. A 1950 survey found only 17,500 Protestant church members out of a population of 620,000. As one woman later stated, "Living in Utah may not have made me a better Christian, but it sure made me a better Presbyterian."[13]

Although the Protestant churches made relatively few converts in Zion, they consoled themselves that their institutional efforts had been well worth the effort. Their early schools emphasized both Bible reading and "Americanization," and this, they argued, gradually nudged Latter-day Saint culture back toward the national mainstream. Whereas in 1860 Utahans mainly celebrated the birthdays of Joseph Smith, Jr. and Brigham Young, leaders of the Church of Jesus Christ of Latter-day Saints, and Pioneer Day (July 24, the day that marked the entrance of the Mormons into the Salt Lake Valley), by 1900, they set off fireworks on July 4 and toasted Washington's and Lincoln's birthdays, as well. In 1935, Westminster College officially noted that the Presbyterian goals had shifted from individual conversion to a steady pressure on Mormon culture in general, pushing it slowly toward national norms.[14] That goal remained in place for the succeeding generations.

As Latter-day Saint scholars have shown, such accommodation did, indeed, take place. By the 1920s, LDS youth began to travel to eastern elite universities to study law, medicine, and engineering. The Great Depression gave the Mormons much favorable national publicity as the group that "took care of its own." The public presentation of LDS theology started to change in the early 1980s when church officials added "Another Testament of Jesus Christ" as the Book of Mormon's sub-title. In a major cover story in 2001, *Newsweek* reported that annual references to Jesus in the *Ensign*, the official monthly publication of the Church of Jesus Christ of Latter-day Saints, increased from five to almost 120 within the last 28 years.[15]

The question—"are the Mormons Christian?"—continues to bring forth heated discussion.[16] Presbyterians and Southern Baptists have officially defined Mormons as being outside the Christian pale, and while not going quite so far, both the United Methodist Church and the Roman Catholic Church now require re-baptism if a Latter-day Saint wishes to become a Methodist or a Catholic. Yet only the most rigid Protestant groups still continue to call Mormonism a cult or to think of it as a "sect." In 2003 on CBS's "60 Minutes," Church President Gordon B. Hinckley bluntly declared to Mike Wallace, "We are not weird."[17]

But essential differences in theology and worldview yet remain, and the Latter-day Saints still consider themselves to be God's chosen people and believe that theirs is the only true Christian church. As the LDS sociologist Armand Mauss has noted, the Latter-day Saints in the future will probably continue to walk a delicate line between their traditional role as cultural outsiders and their newly established position as model representatives of the American middle class.[18] If so, the pioneer teachers of the Utah Protestant parochial school systems must somewhere be smiling their approval.

Health Care

If the construction of Protestant parochial educational systems contained great potential for sectarian conflict, the mainline establishment of healthcare institutions moved in the other direction. From the Civil War era forward, virtually all the hospitals and orphanages in the Mountain West region had roots in some form of religious organization.

Catholic hospitals inaugurated the process. In 1870, the Sisters of Saint Joseph established the institution that later became Tucson's St. Mary's Hospital. Around the same time, the Sisters of Charity opened St. Vincent's Hospital in Santa Fe. These, of course, served the entire community.[19]

The nursing nuns were especially prominent in the rugged mining towns of the northern sub-region. Since the majority of the miners hailed from Roman Catholic or Orthodox Christian backgrounds, the usual procedure was to tax everyone to provide a fund to assist the nursing nuns. The makeshift hospital in Price, Utah, utilized this system, as did Providence Hospital in Wallace, Idaho. After considerable negotiation, the Wallace miners convinced the Sisters of Charity from Spokane to turn a three-story bank building into Providence Hospital in 1892, and henceforth the entire health care system lay in their hands: Sister Joseph served as hospital manager; Sister Peter as druggist; Sister Loretta as bookkeeper; Sisters Rosalia and Mary Louise ran the kitchen; and Sisters Josephine and Harmon served as general workers. The only institution for miles around, Providence served both Catholic and non-Catholic alike.[20]

Much of the early region's impetus for church-sponsored health care came from concern over tuberculosis (TB). In 1900, the "White Plague," as it was termed, claimed over 150,000 people a year. It was easily the nation's leading killer, far ahead of cancer and heart disease. No cure existed until the Second World War, and doctors could only urge sufferers to seek out a high, dry climate. In the early years of the twentieth century, the National Tuberculosis Association estimated that perhaps 2,000 people with TB moved to the Southwest every year.[21]

The entire Mountain West is dotted with church-affiliated health care institutions, many of which began as some form of TB sanitarium. The two largest hospitals in Albuquerque yet today are St. Joseph's and Presbyterian. The Methodists founded Good Samaritan in Phoenix and at least seven other hospitals in Montana. The Baptists also began hospitals in El Paso and Tucson.

The wealthy Episcopal Church proved especially active in this regard. It founded hospitals in Lander and Jackson, Wyoming, as well as a St. Luke's in

Denver and a St. Luke's in Phoenix. The St. Luke's in Boise today shares region-al health care duties with Catholic St. Alphonsus. The Episcopal hospitals in near-by Sioux country usually contained a nurses' training school for Native American women as well.[22]

Concern for TB sufferers also led to the establishment of the National Jewish Hospital in Denver. Brainchild of the region's most prominent Reform rabbi, William S. Friedman, the hospital began in 1892 but closed temporarily with the financial panic of the next year. Seven years later, with aid from the B'nai B'rith Jewish fraternal organization, the hospital opened permanently, and in a dramat-ic gesture charged no fees for TB sufferers. "We did not ask of what nationality or faith they were," Friedman said, "only that they be sick and unable to pay."[23]

The Mormons, too, founded hospitals and other health-care facilities. Under the aegis of the Female Relief Society—whose president Eliza R. Snow (with church president Brigham Young's approval) urged Mormon women to obtain degrees from Eastern medical colleges—established the Deseret Hospital in Salt Lake City. Although short-lived, this medical institution became the first of many LDS medical facilities, many of them financed and staffed by Mormon women. Of particular note is the LDS Primary Children's Hospital that began under the supervision of the Primary Auxiliary, whose female leadership, responsible for the early church training of Mormon children, helped youngsters appreciate the need to support a hospital to care for all the sick children in the community. Eventually the ownership of all LDS health facilities was transferred to the church so that by 1963 the church owned or administered 15 hospitals in the Mountain West.

All these hospitals and other church-sponsored institutions formed a crucial part of the religious life in the Mountain West region. Except in the case of Utah and Idaho, where the issue of polygamy was a complicating factor throughout much of the nineteenth century, the high visibility of these health-care institutions helped dampen organized religious contentiousness because the various denomi-nations were all providing much-needed social services. As the Episcopal Bishop Daniel Tuttle remarked in his *Reminiscences* (1906), "when the church takes the lead in beneficent activities for human welfare, sneering at or capricious criticism of her is never heard."[24]

That this was the case for much of the Mountain West from the 1860s to the mid-twentieth century may be best demonstrated by the presence in Boulder, Colorado of the Colorado Sanitarium, built in 1895 by an outsider group, the Seventh-day Adventists. For well over a half-century, this institution, which was known for its excellent training of student nurses, served patients of all religious persuasions. In 1962, a new building was constructed and the institution was re-named Boulder Memorial Hospital. It was sold to its competitor, the Boulder

Community Hospital, in the 1980s and a new Seventh-day Adventist health facility was constructed in nearby Louisville, Colorado.

The Roller Coaster Mainline Ride from World War II to the Sixties

World War II and the ensuing Cold War introduced major changes in the religious situation in the Mountain West. During the war, churches and synagogues largely emphasized the theme of ecumenicism. Past antagonisms were placed on the back burner as Protestants, Catholics, Jews, and Mormons all viewed Nazi Germany as the intrusion of evil into the historical process. In 1943, for example, a Salt Lake Presbyterian minister proclaimed Jesus as "the world's first democrat," arguing that the founder of Christianity long had championed the downtrodden of all races and all classes, Jews and Gentiles alike. Three years later, the Utah Episcopal Bishop declared that the post-war world would likely be less an "atomic age" than one of internationalism.[25] A number of ecumenical gatherings during the war argued that the churches bore the main responsibility for the future integrity of the nation. They agreed, moreover, that ecumenical cooperation was possible without compromising religious principles or denominational integrity.[26]

The post-war years seemed to bear out these statements. From 1945 to the early 1960s, the cities of the Mountain West—showcased by Denver—underwent a mammoth church building program. A 1950 Denver survey discovered that the Queen City had erected 35 new religious buildings in the previous five years, at a cost of over $1 million. A decade afterward, another survey discovered over 250 new churches and synagogues, costing $2.5 million. Many ministers during these years were like the Salt Lake City Lutheran pastor who remarked in 1957, "Some pastors are called to teaching and counsel; I have been called to build churches."[27] In sociological terms, the mainline religious forces of the era "confirmed" the social order. Only the scattered African-American churches seriously challenged the status quo on matters of race and poverty.

On a national level, the post-war milieu witnessed the "mainstreaming" of Roman Catholicism, but of course, the Southwest had anticipated this by at least two centuries. During the 1950s, the region's Catholic schools achieved their heyday. In terms of cultural power, the Archbishop of New Mexico, Edwin V. Byrne, probably surpassed that of any elected state official.

In the fall of 1952, a relatively obscure event occurred in Dallas, Texas, that would eventually have considerable impact on the religious landscape of the Mountain West. In September of that year, the Southern Baptist Convention officially decided to expand into the region, which, thanks to an early comity agreement with the American (Northern) Baptists, they had generally left to others.

Following the motto "a million more in '54," Southern Baptist missionaries and church extension workers began to follow their former parishioners who had decided to settle in the Mountain region. In addition, they developed an aggressive evangelistic campaign to win new converts. Within two decades, the Southern Baptist Convention suddenly became a powerful social force in the Mountain West. In 1973, Riverside Baptist Church in Denver declared itself the largest Southern Baptist Church outside the Old South. Five years later, First Baptist in Phoenix made an identical claim, noting that it was the largest Baptist church in 29 states. As the historian Daniel Carnett has shown, from 1940 to 1955, New Mexican Southern Baptists rose from a minor denomination to become larger than all the rest of the state's Protestants put together.[28] Most cities in the Mountain West today harbor large Southern Baptist churches, although several have dropped both "southern" and "Baptist" from their official name. In the wake of the Southern Baptist expansion came scores of other independent evangelical churches, all highly skilled in proclaiming their gospel message via print, radio, and television.

The 1960s

Although the mainline pastors and parishioners of the post-war era assumed that their middle-class hegemony would persist indefinitely, this world began to collapse in "the sixties," the decade between 1963 and 1973 that produced cataclysmic shifts in the nation's religious life. Pope John XXIII's calling of the Second Vatican council completely transformed over 450 years of Catholic-Protestant tension by re-categorizing their former antagonists as "separated Brethren" and inaugurating renewed dialogue on a number of fronts. Simultaneously, however, the changes of Vatican II virtually institutionalized dissent within the Catholic Church over such issues as woman priests, birth control, the administering of the sacraments to divorced church members, and married clergy. Two decades later, an even more wrenching crisis over accusations of clerical sex abuse began to rock the powerful church to its very foundations. Attendance at Mass and Confession began to fall, and the church faced a major challenge in recruiting sufficient priests and nuns. As an Irish priest wryly observed in 2000, if the church lost hold of this generation, it would also lose their children, the next; and if that happened, they would need St. Patrick back again.[29]

In 1967, the Six-Day War between Israel and its Arab neighbors not only revealed the fragility of the Jewish state, it also galvanized American Jewish support for Israel. This helped to move the ever-volatile Middle East onto the front desks of the State Department, where it would remain for the rest of the century. But that war did much more. Just as the Holocaust had done for American Jewry, this war intensified Jewish identity throughout the nation. While this process did not necessarily make Jews more observant, it made the Jewish community more visible in the larger community, a development that was as noticeable in the Mountain West as elsewhere.

Although the mainline Protestant churches lacked a comparable dramatic event, they too experienced severe upheavals. Parishioners began to decamp by the thousands as a "crisis of belief" swept through the generation of Baby Boomers. In addition, the traditional mainline suddenly found itself faced with an increasingly high profile conservative evangelical Protestantism that started to see itself as a "New Protestant Establishment." In the Mountain West, this realignment could be seen in two areas: the 1970s arrival of several conservative Protestant groups to the Boise and Colorado Springs areas, showcased by the latter's Focus on the Family Center (founded in 1977); and the gigantic crowds—well over 50,000—that attended the Denver-based Promise Keepers' rallies all through the region in the 1990s. Suddenly the historic Protestant mainline simply was not mainline any more.

Sociologists of religion have tried to put these dramatic changes into perspective. Some maintain that post-modern America was experiencing a "secularization" à la Europe, where the majestic Cathedrals are still valued for their architectural splendor but are generally absent of worshippers. Others, however, strongly disagree, arguing that Europe is the anomaly and that faith in America had simply become "democratized." From about 1965 forward, every man and woman has assumed the role of private theologian, as witnessed in the current catch phrase—now virtually a cliché—"I'm not religious, but I'm very spiritual."

Parallel with the democratization of faith came the famed "lifestyle revolution," encompassing such hot-button issues as homosexual rights, abortion, drug use, and out-of-wedlock births. As the sociologists Robert Wuthnow and James Davison Hunter have argued, these crises have produced a virtual realignment of the nation's religious landscape.[30] With some exceptions, Unitarians on one side and hard-line conservative evangelicals and Mormons on the other, the lines of division usually cut right through most denominations. Traditionally liberal Protestants, Catholics, and Jews tried and continue to try to bend traditional biblical and historic teachings to encompass some of the current social shifts, whereas conservative Protestants, Catholics, and Jews maintain that traditional biblical teachings are revealed by God, and thus are as valid now as they ever were. This realignment has produced some strange bedfellows. When the Archbishop of New Mexico, Michael Sheehan, led a march against an Albuquerque Planned Parenthood clinic in December 2002, he might well have passed out literature from the conservative evangelical Focus on the Family, for they hold almost identical views on the abortion question.[31]

An unexpected consequence of this "culture wars" atmosphere, in the words of Father Richard John Neuhaus, has been to create a "naked public square." If religious values do not fill the public square, he argues, the secular state will supply them by default, and the result, inevitably, will be social chaos.[32] In the post-modern era, as the saying goes, God gives humanity free will; the state decides what is legal; and the church and synagogue provide rules about what is right.

A good many bitter squabbles in what Wuthnow has termed the "struggle for America's soul"[33] have been played out on the canvas of the Mountain West. These struggles include:

- A dramatic 1953 raid by the Arizona state police on a splinter Mormon polygamous community in the Arizona Strip town of Short Creek (now known as Colorado City) that engendered a great deal of unfavorable publicity and essentially proved the last of its kind;
- Various conservative evangelical crusades of the 1970s-1990s that came within a whisker of electing an anti-evolution majority to the Los Alamos, New Mexico school board and engendered bitter election fights in Colorado Springs over gay rights legislation;
- Periodic police stand-offs with extremist para-military/religious groups in the 1990s in Idaho and Montana;
- The reaction to the brutal 1998 murder of the gay college student Matthew Shepard in Laramie, Wyoming, because of his sexual orientation;
- The reaction to horrific murders the following year at Columbine High School in Colorado by troubled Satanist youth.

And so on.

The international appeal of Sedona, Arizona, and Roswell, New Mexico, as "alternative religious sites" operates on a far more subdued and considerably more popular level. By the 1980s, Sedona's marvelous red rock and pine tree backdrop, plus its reputation as a spiritual "power spot," had turned it into a mecca for religious seekers from around the globe. It became, in the words of the *Los Angeles Times*, "the Vatican City of the New Age Movement," or as the sociologist Adrian J. Ivakhiv describes it, a spot where seekers can confront the "non-human Other" on an individual basis.[34] Even the AAA guidebook to Arizona notes that Sedona "is purportedly home to several vortexes, electromagnetic energy fields emitting upward from earth…[that] are thought to energize and inspire visitors."[35] Native American protests that New Age "shamans" are co-opting their historic spiritual traditions for profit and U.S. Park Service and Forest Service complaints over the sudden appearance of stone circles in isolated locations have had virtually no impact on the popularity of this crusade. Sedona is now second only to the Grand Canyon as the most visited site in Arizona.

Similarly, the alleged crash of an unidentified flying object in Roswell, New Mexico, in July 1947 has been transformed from a minor Cold War incident into a major quasi-spiritual industry, supplemented by hundreds of sightings on the Great Plains of the Dakotas and Montana. Composed equally of true believers and indignant skeptics, the UFO phenomenon reflects many of the religious dilemmas of the modern age. It asks the question "are we alone?" that science cannot really answer, with some observers suggesting that UFOs seem to be playing the role of modern angels.[36]

These incidents have all occurred in the Mountain West for some excellent sociological reasons. The last half-century has seen such cities as Phoenix, Tucson, Albuquerque, Colorado Springs, Fort Collins, and Boise grow from small towns into sprawling metropolitan areas, bringing the anonymity, anomie, and attendant social dislocations that often accompany such transformations. Great wealth has blessed such high-tech communities as Los Alamos, Boulder, Boise, and Colorado Springs, but nearby rural areas struggle through long winters marked by abject poverty and horrific environmental degradation. In addition, the lack of population and open space provide opportunities for a variety of communal groups—from the respected Sikhs in Española, New Mexico, to various millennialist extremists—to carry out their various programs.

The Mainstream Reacts to the New Milieu

In general, the historic mainstream Protestant denominations, as well as liberal to moderate Catholics, Jews, and even Latter-day Saints, seem somewhat bewildered by these recent shifts. All through the region, the mainline Protestant, Catholic, and Reform and Conservative Jewish clerics and their congregations have emphasized interfaith cooperation and have consistently led local opposition to various extremist sects. The Elizabeth Smart kidnapping case, with its tragic connections to polygamy and Mormon fundamentalism, placed public emphasis on how the Church of Jesus Christ of Latter-day Saints opposes Mormonism's own peculiar form of religious extremism.

In the wake of the Laramie and Columbine murders, clerical representatives of the region's several religious mainstreams all made efforts to heal their troubled communities. In the instance of the appalling murders of the dozen high-school students in Littleton, Colorado however, the conservative evangelical currents sweeping through many of the region's metropolitan areas overshadowed the efforts at extending comfort and solace that were made by the clerical members of the Interfaith Alliance of Colorado such as its president, the Rev. Michael Carrier, a Denver Presbyterian pastor, the Rev. Patrick Demmer, president of the mostly black Greater Metro Denver Ministerial Alliance, the Catholic Archbishop Charles Chaput, and Rabbi Fred Greenspahn of Littleton's Temple Beth Shalom.

Andrew Walsh's account in *Religion and the News* (Summer 1999) reveals how Franklin Graham (son of the famed evangelist Billy Graham) and local evangelical leaders took ownership of the historic clerical task of leading public mourning in times of catastrophic disruption of the ordinary rhythms of existence. In this stunning piece, Walsh developed a template that serves as a means of measuring the public shift away from the growing tolerance of difference (and even otherness) that had started to characterize American religion not only in the Mountain West but also throughout the nation in the second half of the twentieth century.

Evidence of the distrust and perhaps even fear of difference/otherness on the part of conservatives in many religious communities has been revealed in recent years by the very public opposition to the growing cultural acceptance of gays and lesbians in all sectors of society. Almost no denomination has escaped disagreement and sometimes fierce public argument about how appropriate it is, or would be, for gays and lesbians to be ordained as clerical leaders. Many conservatives, however, go much further. In disapproving the very existence of gays, lesbians, and transgendered persons, they conclude that homosexuality is a "lifestyle choice," a character flaw that can be remedied through human effort and psychological treatment.

A more common religious reaction—the one taken by the Latter-day Saints and by much of the regional Catholic community—is "hate the sin but love the sinner." This is a position that recognizes the reality of homosexuality, but calls on homosexual persons to refrain from any overt expression of their sexual nature. In response to such positions, which they regard as both mistaken and intolerant, the Unitarians, Congregationalists [United Church of Christ], and many Episcopalian congregations in the Mountain West have become "Open and Affirming," thereby indicating that gay, lesbian, and transgender members are welcome and are encouraged to become a part of these communities.

Rather than denouncing their opponents, the mainstream churches and synagogues have in large measure marched steadily along their familiar historic paths: providing services, as they see the need, to both parishioners and to the community at large. In the modern era, however, one sees a subtle difference in approach. Although the mainline denominations continue to construct churches and the occasional camp or retirement home, the emphasis rests less on creating institutions than on creating various religious *programs*. And these, although perhaps less permanent, and certainly less flashy, reflect the continual mainstream commitment to the betterment of regional life.

The denominations have proven quite innovative in this regard. In 1979, the Episcopal Church in Utah dedicated in Salt Lake City the state's first apartment building designed for the elderly and the handicapped. The Evangelical Lutherans and the Congregationalists have combined to establish an extensive set of retirement homes all through the West. Drawing on the traditional African-American concern for social issues, the Pueblo African Methodist Episcopal Church opened a Free Store in the mid-1970s. An Episcopal rector in Salt Lake City donned the mantle of "motel chaplain" for the city's Holiday Inn, dealing with a solid middle-class clientele that share such universal dilemmas as job loss, alcoholism, and unwanted pregnancies.

In the mid-1960s a consortium of Denver's Protestant clerics, including the pastor of the First Spanish Methodist Church, began an ecumenical inner city parish to respond to downtown Denver's rapid social decay. For years these clerics served as much as social workers as they did as traditional clergy. During this time, Denver's historic Trinity Methodist Church fended off possible closure by reaching out to all segments of the inner city: it became home to the Denver Chamber Orchestra and offered classes in computing and ballroom dancing. At the other end of the social spectrum, it also provided a 24-hour ministry, complete with AA counseling and a job-placement service, to the steady stream of the homeless who filed past its doors.

In the rural countryside, the small Catholic and Protestant churches also continued their historic involvement. The rural areas all faced similar dilemmas: poverty, lack of employment, and the steady exodus of young people. The clerics responded as best they could. For example, from 1984-1991, northern New Mexico Methodist pastor Jesse Hodge and his wife Liz introduced the following programs: flag football for grade schoolers (200 participated); girls' basketball program (93 participated); a rejuvenated cancer support group; a Meals on Wheels for the homebound; and an expensive, specially equipped van to transport the handicapped and the aged.[37] In nearby Clayton, Father John C. Bragher bolstered existing social programs and became the Catholic representative for the Tri-State Ministerial Alliance. Whether these programs continued under their successors cannot be determined.

In both rural and urban areas, the mainline church basements housed an endless variety of support groups: Alcoholics Anonymous, Overeaters Anonymous, Mothers Against Drunk Driving, etc., as well as the more traditional Boy Scouts, Girl Scouts, and Campfire programs. Numerous church-run pre-schools, day-care centers, and after-hours child-care programs also dot most contemporary Mountain West cities today.

Few would deny the worth of these mainstream socio-religious efforts. Although the various levels of government have generally assumed responsibility for social welfare, schooling, and health care needs, unfortunately human dilemmas regularly outrun the resources of any official governmental agency. Thus, the mainline "outsider" witness to the Mountain West has maintained a continuity for over 150 years.

Conclusion

At the onset of the twenty-first century, the religious landscape of the Mountain West bears a striking resemblance to the situation that first greeted the mainline incomers of the 1850s. One finds Native American groups whose communities manifest both syncretic Christian/Native faiths as well as more traditional perspectives. The American Indian Religious Freedom Act of 1978 guaranteed indigenous groups the right "to believe, express and exercise traditional religions," and the Native American Graves Protection and Repatriation Act 12 years later insured that many Native American sacred objects held by museums would be retuned to the tribes of origin. Moreover, the long-standing Native concern for the environment has increasingly received a wide regional backing.

One also finds a still powerful Spanish Catholic quasi-establishment in the Southwest, but over time it has learned to share its cultural hegemony with Hispanic Protestant churches as well as those of the mainline. The unique feature of the region, of course, is a prospering, quasi-establishment in Mormon Utah that has moved closer to the national mainstream but still marches to its own drummer.

There is also a growing conservative evangelical presence in all the small towns and large cities, with an especially high visibility in Wyoming and Colorado Springs, as well as a fading ethnic church consciousness on the Great Plains, and thriving counter-cultural havens in Sedona, Santa Fe, and Boulder.

Overall, one meets a region-wide variegated Protestant-Catholic-Jewish presence that continues to provide needed spiritual and social services, but seems to be searching for a theological place to stand; and everywhere one hears concern over quality of life, social problems, and environmental issues that seem to defy easy solution. In some regions there is theological peace, while in others the religious tension is almost palpable.

Can this religio-cultural diversity ever recapture the (relative) tranquility that characterized the era that stretched from 1940 to 1963? To answer this, one might paraphrase a recent speech by the eminent Catholic theologian, Hans Kung: there can be no regional tranquility without peace among the major religious groups of the area; there can be no peace among the religious groups without meaningful dialogue; and there can be no meaningful dialogue without some understanding of minimal ethical standards.[38] That, in a nutshell, is the challenge that confronts all the religious forces in the Mountain West today.

Endnotes

1. Jake Page, ed., *Sacred Lands of Indian America*, Photography by David Meunch, foreword by Charles E. Little (New York: Harry N. Abrams, 1999).
2. Robert Hickman Adams, *White Churches of the Plains: Examples from Colorado* (Boulder: The Colorado Associated University Press, 1970).
3. See "Once They Flourished: Denver's Former Synagogues," *L'Chaim to Lite—Intermountain Jewish News* (September 14, 1990): 21-27; quotation on 22. Henry J. Tobias, *The Jews of New Mexico* (Albuquerque: University of New Mexico Press, 1990); and Harriet Rochlin and Fred Rochlin, *Pioneer Jews: New Life in the Far West* (Boston: Houghton Mifflin, 1959).
4. The best biography is Paul Horgan, *Lamy of Santa Fe* (New York: Farrar, Straus, and Giroux, 1975).
5. Erin Whalen, "Loretto Academy Remembered," *Las Cruces Sun-News* (Feb. 28, 1982).
6. *El Abogado Cristiano* (October 1907).
7. Quoted in Edith J. Agnew and Ruth K. Barber, "The Unique Presbyterian School System of New Mexico," *Journal of Presbyterian History* 49 (Fall, 1921): 205.
8. Jan Shipps, *Mormonism: The Story of a New Religious Tradition* (Urbana: University of Illinois Press, 1985).
9. W.M. Barrows to A.H. Clapp, April 2, 1877, American Home Missionary Society Papers; reel 244. Annual Report Upon Domestic Missions of the Protestant Episcopal Church, 1891, 5.
10. See Ferenc Morton Szasz, *The Protestant Clergy in the Great Plains and Mountain West, 1865-1916* (Albuquerque: University of New Mexico Press, 1988).
11. Mark T. Banker, *Presbyterian Missions and Cultural Interaction in the Far Southwest, 1850-1950* (Urbana: University of Illinois Press, 1993); Sarah Deutsch, *No Separate Refuge* (New York: Oxford University Press, 1987); and Randi Jones Walker, *Protestantism in the Sangre de Cristos, 1850-1920* (Albuquerque: University of New Mexico Press, 1991).
12. Sidney E. Mead, *The Nation With the Soul of a Church* (New York: Harper's, 1975), and Mead, *The Old Religion in the Brave New World: Reflections on the Relation Between Christendom and the Republic* (Berkeley: University of California Press, 1977).
13. See Herbert W. Reherd, "An Outline History of the Protestant Churches in Utah," in W. Wain Sutton, ed., *Utah: A Centennial History* vol. 2 (1949). The woman prefers to remain anonymous.
14. Szasz, *Protestant Clergy*, Chapter 7; Daniel S. Tuttle, *Reminiscences of a Missionary Bishop* (New York: Thomas Whittaker, 1906), 314.
15. *Newsweek*, Sept. 10, 2001.
16. See Jan Shipps, "'Is Mormonism Christian?' Reflections on a Complicated Question," *BYU Studies* 33 (1993).
17. *Newsweek*, Sept. 10, 2001.

18. Armand L. Mauss, *The Angel and the Beehive: The Mormon Struggle with Assimilation* (Urbana: University of Illinois Press, 1994).
19. Ferenc Morton Szasz, *Religion in the Modern American West* (Tucson: University of Arizona Press, 2000), Chapter 1.
20. Pamphlet "Providence Hospital," acquired in Wallace, Idaho. Copy in author's possession.
21. See Jake W. Spidle, Jr., "An Army of Tubercular Invalids: New Mexico and the Birth of the Tuberculosis Industry," *New Mexico Historical Review* 61 (July 1986): 179-201.
22. The Episcopal church was very active in this line. See Ferenc Morton Szasz, "Episcopal Bishops and the Trans-Mississippi West, 1865-1915," *Anglican and Episcopal History* LXIX (September 2000): 348-370.
23. *Denver Republican*, Jan. 24, 1899; March 18, 1899.
24. Tuttle, *Reminiscences*, 205.
25. *Salt Lake City Tribune*, June 13, 1943; *Salt Lake City Tribune*, June 17, 1946.
26. *Newsletter*, National Conference of Christians and Jews (1944), copy, Oklahoma Historical Society, Oklahoma City, Oklahoma.
27. "Religions of Salt Lake City," typescript, Utah Historical Society, Salt Lake City, Utah.
28. Daniel Carnett, *A History of New Mexico Baptists, 1939-1995* (Albuquerque: University of New Mexico Press, 2002).
29. *Irish Times*, Aug. 21, 2000. Copy, Dublin Central Library, Dublin, Ireland.
30. Robert Wuthnow, *The Restructuring of American Religion: Society and Faith since World War II* (Princeton, N.J.: Princeton University Press, 1988); James Davison Hunter, *Culture Wars: The Struggle to Define America* (New York: Basic Books, 1991).
31. *Albuquerque Sunday Journal*, Dec. 30, 2001; *Focus on the Family: Who We Are and What We Stand For* (Pamphlet 1991), 10-11.
32. Richard John Neuhaus, *The Naked Public Square: Religion and Democracy in America* (Grand Rapids, Mich.: William B. Eerdman's, 1989).
33. Robert Wuthnow, *The Struggle for America's South: Evangelicals, Liberals, and Secularism* (Grand Rapids, Mich.: William B. Eerdman's, 1989).
34. Adrian J. Ivakhiv, *Claiming Sacred Ground: Pilgrims and Politics at Glastonbury and Sedona* (Bloomington and Indianapolis: Indiana University Press, 2001).
35. *AAA Tourbook: Arizona and New Mexico* (Florida: AAA Publications, 2000), 91.
36. The best book on the religious aspect of this phenomenon is Brenda Denzler, *The Lure of the Edge: Scientific Passions, Religious Beliefs, and the Pursuit of UFOs* (Berkeley: University of California Press, 2001). See also Paul Devereux and Peter Brookesmith, UFOs and Ufology: the First 50 Years (London: Blandford, 1997).
37. *Raton Range*, June 7, 1991.
38. Kung's speech, given in Dublin, was entitled "Global Ethic—A Vision for the Twenty-First Century," *Irish Times*, May 5, 2000.

CHAPTER THREE

CATHOLIC HEARTLAND IN TRANSITION: ARIZONA AND NEW MEXICO

Randi Jones Walker[1]

N ew Mexico and Arizona are home to some of the oldest religious communities and traditions in the United States—and some of the newest. When mission Catholicism and Spanish civil authority entered the area in the sixteenth century, they found long-established native cultures already in place. Altering without entirely obliterating the religious dimensions of those cultures, priests and powerful secular figures put deep roots down that produced both a religious establishment in the European manner of that time and a sub-regional Catholic culture that endured well into the twentieth century. Successive waves of migration complicated the situation, gradually altering both the religious and the secular cultures. But these alterations occurred in such disparate fashion that, while these two states form a sub-region of the Mountain West, New Mexico and Arizona are now quite dissimilar.

Arizona increasingly resembles southern California, especially in its metropolitan areas: Scottsdale, Glendale, Mesa, and Phoenix are included in the *2003 World Almanac's* list of the "10 fastest-growing big cities" in the nation. In New Mexico, the Albuquerque metropolitan area is also increasing in population. But there is considerable discrepancy in the rate of population growth in these two states. Between 1990 and 2000, New Mexico's population rate increased only half as fast as that of Arizona. This difference reflects not only the addition of smaller numbers of people to the population, but also a slower rate of cultural change.

As it nearly always does, religion stands at the heart of cultural change in this sub-region. While numbers never tell the full story, a good place to start is with the extent of religious affiliation. The contemporary difference in the percentage of churched and unchurched people in these two states is as remarkable as the difference in growth rates. Data from the North American Religion Atlas (NARA) reveal that Arizona is among the least churched states in the nation. Fifty-nine percent of its population are unaffiliated or uncounted by any religious body. New Mexico, by contrast, is among the more "churched" states in the nation. Only 37 percent of its people are not counted as adherents of some religious body. That proportion probably should be even lower since, unless they are Roman Catholics or members of some Protestant body, Native Americans, whose ethnicity is by and large their religious affiliation, are not counted as adherents to organized religious bodies.

The critical religious story in these two states, however, is not the level of religious affiliation or the lack of connection to religious bodies. In truth, those levels have not changed appreciably in the past two decades.[2] Using a longer baseline for comparison purposes, the most remarkable religious story in this subregion is a dramatic fluctuation in the Catholic population in New Mexico and a significant decline in the percentage of Catholics within the total of religious adherents in Arizona.

Although less precise than the numbers for "adherents" as defined in the NARA data, Catholics and most of the nation's Protestant organizations report "membership" statistics to the National Council of Churches (NCC) annually, and they have been doing so since the early years of the twentieth century. The NCC's 1950 report indicates that, at mid-century, 68 percent of the total church membership in New Mexico was Roman Catholic. In Arizona, the percentage was 54.7. Such elevated proportions of Catholics in the religious mix in these two states support accounts of their histories that indicate that Roman Catholicism, the legally established church until the area became U.S. territory in 1848, continued as a virtual establishment well into the twentieth century. Although organized Protestant bodies as well as Mormons have long been in the area, Catholics have usually been a majority and have always been a plurality within the religious community in both states. But robust numbers are not what made the real difference. Roman Catholicism exercised cultural power that rested on its long history of being *the* church.

The general perception is that the Catholic Church is still "the" church. By 1980, however, the percentage of Catholics in the total adherent pool had decreased from 68 to 56.7 percent in New Mexico and from 54.7 percent to less than half—45.2 percent—in Arizona. This precipitous Catholic decline appears even sharper if it is viewed another way: whereas two out of three people in the population of New Mexico were Catholic in 1950, only one out of every three was Catholic in 1980. More than half the people in Arizona were Roman Catholic in 1950; in 1980 that number had dropped to 40 percent.

In the last two decades of the twentieth century this decline was halted in New Mexico to some degree. Instead of the surprisingly low 1980 figure of a third of the state's population being Roman Catholic, four out of every 10 people were Catholic adherents in 2000. From the perspective of the number of Catholics in the state's total number of religious adherents, the Catholic percentage was up to 58.4. This, of course, does not approach the proportion reported in 1950. Yet it is trending upward. This may mean that the church's quasi-establishment status stands a chance of being reclaimed in New Mexico. But only if—and this is a good-sized if—the impact of the recent clerical scandals can be overcome.

In Arizona, the numbers indicate that the loss of Catholic hegemony is not temporary. From considerably more than half of all religious adherents in the state in 1950, the percentage declined to 45.2 percent in 1980 and dipped again to 43.2 in 2000.[3] Although these are not large percentage declines, they continue to move downward. Of much greater import, the percentage of Catholics in the total population has decreased by over half. In 1980, 40 percent of the people in Arizona were Catholics; in 2000, that proportion had declined to 19 percent.

Exactly how much this whittling away of Catholic predominance has to do with politics in this sub-region is a very complicated question. Once it was a truism that Catholics voted Democratic in national elections while Protestants, especially conservative Protestants, were Republican. While this no longer holds, it stands to reason that the general political landscape is not totally unconnected to what is happening to organized religion in these two states. In both states, there are movements that "spiritualize" the environment, making concern for natural surroundings as much a religious duty as building and caring for chapels, churches, cathedrals, and sanctuaries of all kinds. This is having a political impact. In addition, the political landscape is also affected by large numbers of "Nones" in the population, particularly in Arizona.

In presidential elections, the Republican Party tends to count Arizona as fairly safe even though it voted for Bill Clinton by a narrow majority in 1996. Reflecting its strong Catholic majority, New Mexico supported Democrats in the 1992, 1996, and 2000 elections. But political conservatism is regarded as such a hallmark of this sub-region that predicting how elections will turn out is difficult.

Actually, this sub-region may not be as rigidly conservative as some seem to think. Nationally, public policy issues related to religion in the United States include abortion, gay rights, environmental protection, school vouchers, national health insurance, and governmental assistance to minorities, as well as a role for government in fighting poverty. That these issues concern religious people in Arizona and New Mexico is shown in studies tracking the influence of religion on political partisanship and ideology conducted at the Bliss Institute. But the data from the outcome of the Institute's national surveys reveal that, on these issues, this sub-region appears to be only slightly more conservative than the rest of the nation.[4]

There are, however, other distinctive issues of public policy that attract intense attention from religious people in both states. These include the role of religion in the public schools; the right of Native Americans to full religious freedom; the role of the Roman Catholic Church in political life; environmental issues focused on toxic waste disposal, the location of power plants, strip mining, and nuclear energy activities; and the role of the federal government in land use policy for Arizona and New Mexico. Many of these more or less local issues are of long standing. When they come up in public debate, religious concerns are often brought to the fore. But when this happens, the influence of that substantial part of the population unaffiliated with any religious body also makes itself heard. In taking political positions that are essentially libertarian, this population segment often challenges positions reflecting an older understanding of the sub-region as a land of Protestant conservatism and Catholic quasi-establishment.

Although it is true that the religious profiles of New Mexico and Arizona are now diverging, areas with distinct geographies are shared by the two states, and in each one of these areas, distinctive cultures reflect multiple layers of settlement. Because all are noticeably different, and those differences help to shape the religious ambiance of each area, it is impossible to adequately describe religion and public life in this sub-region without taking geography and the history of settlement into account. Since most of these geographical areas cross state boundaries, however, the political impact of religion is easier to detect at the local rather than state and national levels.

Desert landscapes, red rock formations, isolated fertile valleys, and enormous distances between settlements mark the Colorado Plateau, the most northern of these areas. Stretching southward from Utah and Colorado across the northern part of both Arizona and New Mexico, this area is home to Native Americans who, for a long time, made up most of the population. Hopi and Zuni people came first, and Navajo, Ute, and Apache people came later, but both tribal groupings have lived there for centuries. Until the early twentieth century when Farmington and Flagstaff and other small cities began to grow, these two native populations were very much in the majority.

Movies and popular literature, especially Tony Hillerman's Navajo detective novels, shape the religio-ethnic landscape of the Colorado Plateau in the American imagination. The general perception seems to be that the Plateau is almost entirely peopled by Native Americans whose religion is the traditional Indian way. There is no statistical way to check out this perception, since NARA data do not include Native American, First Nations, or tribal religions. If Indian religions are represented at all, they are hidden among the unaffiliated or uncounted adherents, of which there are many in the counties of the Colorado Plateau. Therefore, the best way to determine adherence to these religions is to draw inferences from comparisons of the American Indian population variable in the U.S. Census and the NARA religious adherence variables. While some American Indians are either members of the Roman Catholic Church or some Protestant body, such a comparison strongly suggests that what Hillerman calls the Navajo Way and other traditional Indian religious beliefs and practices are alive and well on the Colorado Plateau.[5]

In addition to Native Americans, the Arizona and New Mexico section of the Colorado Plateau is home to Anglo-Americans who came to work in mining, power plants, or the tourist industry.[6] They probably bring histories of Christian affiliations with them, but the size and number of congregations in the Plateau area suggest that not many affiliate with local Catholic or Protestant congregations.

Over the last 100 years, the Church of Jesus Christ of Latter-day Saints developed an ever stronger presence in this area, both among Anglos and Native Americans. The Colorado Plateau is also home to several groups of "Mormon fundamentalists," people who believe that Mormon doctrines continue to call for the practice of plural marriage. Colorado City, in the isolated area known as the Arizona Strip, is home to the largest of these groups.

The plains of eastern and northern New Mexico form a second geographical area. They are extensions of the west Texas ranch lands, a fact reflected in their economy and culture. Because Anglo ranchers have largely displaced the former Native Americans and Hispanic residents, Bible Belt religious traditions predominate. Conservative evangelical—especially small Baptist, Holiness, and Pentecostal—and historic Protestant mainline churches dot the landscape, accounting for the majority of the congregations in this geographical area. But Catholicism still accounts for more than 20 percent of the population.

The mountains of northern and southern New Mexico and central and eastern Arizona form another distinct geographical area. It has scattered Hispanic communities, many dating from Spanish colonial days, along with towns populated by more recent Anglo and/or Mexican-American immigrants. Small Roman Catholic churches predominate here, among them the oldest churches in the United States. In addition, there are a few Protestant churches that were founded over a 100 years ago, as well as growing numbers of newer Holiness and Pentecostal congregations. The Sangre de Cristos in northern New Mexico and the Mogollon Rim and the White Mountains in Arizona also contain sites long sacred to the Native American peoples, some of which like Chimayó, New Mexico have developed into multi-layered spiritual focal points.

The Rio Grande valley, the fourth of these geographical areas, has several layers of culture and religious life. The oldest communities, the Pueblo peoples, maintain native religious practices they brought with them when they moved into the valley 700 or 800 years ago. But in many—perhaps most—Pueblos, elements of Roman Catholic Christianity were superimposed over the native traditions. The area is organized into Catholic parishes, but most of the parishioners practice both religions side by side, or some mixture of the two traditions. Their ethnic identity is Native American; their religious identity is Roman Catholic. In short, they are Indian Catholics.

The Anglo population in this geographical area has gradually increased over the past 150 years. In recent decades, especially in the cities of Albuquerque, Las Cruces, El Paso (a border city in Texas that spills over into New Mexico and old Mexico as well) and even Sante Fe, the size of the non-Indian population has grown steadily. The resulting concentration of Anglos accounts for the presence of many Protestant congregations in these cities. Until very recently, however, the religious population retained a slight Roman Catholic majority, and, except for the unaffiliated, Roman Catholics remain the largest single religious group in this area.

The Gila River valley in southern Arizona and the southern Colorado River valley, the most Anglo and the fastest growing part of the Arizona-New Mexico sub-region, is the other distinct geographical area. Located entirely within the boundaries of Arizona, it is so much more closely related culturally to Southern California than to the rest of the region that it makes for exceptions to almost any generalization that could be made about the Arizona-New Mexico region as a whole. Anyone wanting to understand the religious landscape of Phoenix and Tucson would do well to look at the Southern California relationship.

Just as in Southern California, the percentage of Jews in this area is higher than usual for the United States.[7] NARA data also reveal a high percentage of evangelical Protestants, making the "southernization of religion" as pronounced here as it is in Southern California. A growing, largely Christian population of retired people has created its own religious communities, mirroring the communities from which these people came but often lacking the generational diversity or deep common histories of the churches they left behind. The overshadowing religious reality of the Gila valley region, however, is the number of people who are not involved in any organized religious group or do not claim any particular religious practice.

If disparate geographical areas with distinct cultures are one characteristic of the Arizona-New Mexico sub-region, another is the persistence of earlier religious communities in the midst of surprisingly modern cultural overlays of high technology, secularization, and increasingly individualistic New Age explorations of alternative and exotic spiritualities. While some geographical areas such as the Rio Grande valley have more cultural and religious layers and thus thicker histories, others such as the Phoenix suburbs have only single layers with short histories. Yet even where the layers are thin, the proximity to other older religious traditions makes mixing so easy that issues of syncretism arise in nearly all the traditions in the area.

The sub-region's cultural layering rests on Native American religious bedrock. Many tribal groupings settled in the area, some in the desert and others in the valleys of the Colorado and Rio Grande rivers. The cultures of the desert and river valley Pueblos differed (and continue to differ) somewhat, but their religious practices have similarities in that they are all focused on the ordering of human society and its relationship with the natural world. Specific ceremonies maintain each community's relationship to powers, understood to be supernatural, that provide healing for the sick and supply needed moral guidance. For each Pueblo, certain places are sacred. Some are natural; others are created and organized within the Pueblo itself.

Even as the Pueblo people were settling into their current locations, a group of completely different Indian cultures began to migrate into the area. The Navajo and Apache, related cultures originating in the far north, and the Comanches, Utes, and others moving west from the Great Plains, all migrated into territory previously inhabited only by the Pueblos. The religious practices of these new groups varied. All had the predictable religious concern with the community's well being and its relationship to the natural world that sustained it. But the newcomers had a less organized and more individual character than the religions of the Pueblos.

The resulting intersection of the several religious communities in a shared landscape fostered exchange on the one hand and conflict on the other. In order to teach the children, the Navajo took up the Pueblo practice of making dolls that represent the supernatural figures in their religious system, for instance. The various tribal groupings shared an interest in the ability of the others to have access to effective religious or healing power. Inevitably, conflicts generated competition for resources, and vast differences in cultural styles exacerbated the antagonism among the tribes. The Pueblos, settled agricultural people, were vulnerable to the migratory and sometimes predatory ways of the newcomers who sought to make themselves at home and even to exercise dominion over their older neighbors.

This intra-Indian culture clash is an example of the way latecomers construct for themselves a religious sense of belonging. Using a religious vision or idea, they explain that they were placed in the territory bounded by the four mountains by powers greater than themselves, that they belong there, and ought to stay.[8] This example is Native American, but it demonstrates a pervasive pattern that has developed in the religious dynamics of Arizona and New Mexico. Each new group in some sense lays claim to inhabit the land based on a religious view of a granted prerogative. The sense of "divine" entitlement each culture holds makes it difficult to avoid or to adjudicate competing claims and conflicts in their public interactions.

This difficulty played itself out in the southern part of both states, an area that is home to several groups related to the Aztec people of central Mexico as well as the Pueblo peoples of the Rio Grande valley. Never has there been any clear understanding among the sub-region's tribal groupings about who has ownership of native religious sites (and even native religious practices). From time to time, intra-cultural disputes erupted; after the area became part of the United States these intra-cultural disputes often entered the legal system. One of the most famous of these clashes came over Blue Mountain, an area where both Navajo and Hopi people have sacred sites. Government involvement in this dispute goes all the way back to the nineteenth century, but it proved so intractable that it heated up again in the 1970s. In 1986, Congress passed a bill (HR4281) declaring that the area ostensibly shared by the Hopi and Navajo peoples would be divided between the tribes. In order to make this possible, the bill mandated the removal of about 10,000 Navajo from the Hopi part of the former joint use area.

The religious dimensions of this ancient dispute continue to make news. The *Navajo Times* recently reported a dispute involving Navajo families living on the Hopi reservation. The Hopi allege that the Navajo families facing eviction had deliberately defaced a shrine located in the area. The Navajo protested that their ancestors lived in this land, given to them by their creator and marked by four mountains. Believing they also had a right to live there, they sued, generating headlines like the one in the *Tucson Citizen* reporting that "Navajos sue Hopis on Religious Grounds."

The clashes are not always intra-cultural, since the question of whether native practices may be appropriated by non-Indians has also never been settled. This question was addressed in the enormously popular books of Carlos Casteñeda, an author who wrote an anthropological work about a Yaqui shaman, leaving the matter of whether he was writing truth or fiction unclear.[9] The enthusiastic reception Casteñeda's work received illustrates the popularity of Indian traditions with the general public. It also highlights the unanswered question of whether persons other than the members of particular tribes have a right to use Native American rituals in worship.

Anglo commercialization of Native religion is found everywhere in Arizona and New Mexico. Throughout both states, mass-produced Native religious artifacts and symbols are used decoratively. Items with Native American religious symbols on them are for sale everywhere as souvenirs or as art. In addition, easy-to-find advertisements by persons who put themselves forward as Indian religious leaders and shamans willing to teach their practices for a fee illuminate the tension and conflict that is created between those who think Native American religious traditions belong to everyone and those who think such traditions belong only to tribal members of particular Indian cultures.

As they lost control of much of the area to which they once had free access, disputes between Native Americans and private landowners or the United States government developed regarding access to Indian sacred sites.[10] When these disputes reached the courts they were often argued as more or less simple questions of access to public lands with little or no appreciation of how fundamentally religious they were. One reason for this is that the Pueblo peoples and other Indian tribes make efforts to keep sacred sites secret, lest they become the focus of conflict.[11]

One instance from a great multiplicity of attempts made by Native Americans to protect their sacred sites is the current effort Indians are making to prevent the city of Albuquerque from extending a main city street through the Petroglyph National Park, a previously isolated National Monument containing artifacts and sacred sites. For several years, Senator Pete Dominici and Albuquerque Mayor Martin Chavez have made efforts to build the street. Native Americans from several of the Pueblos are mounting a protest to this proposition, but their protests are hampered by the fact that the Pueblo Indians are reluctant to describe the ceremonies they conduct at these sites because they must be kept secret from all except members of the tribe.[12]

Another example of what some see as the struggle between "progress" and protecting Indian sacred sites developed in the late 1980s when the University of Arizona proposed building an observatory on nearby Mt. Graham. As recounted in the *High Country News* (July 24, 1995), a 10-year battle developed between Apache tribal members and environmentalists on one side and scientists and the university on the other. In a letter of protest early in the conflict, the Indians said, "Since time immemorial, Mount Graham has been a sacred mountain to the Apache people." But the powers in charge did not listen and moved ahead to build the first of several multi-million dollar telescopes that would make the Mount Graham International Observatory the home of the largest telescope in the world.[13] Yet another highly publicized effort to protect Native American sacred sites is the Taos effort to recover possession of a sacred lake in the Sangre de Cristo Mountains.[14]

The interaction of natural environment and religion is also pronounced here, though it is by no means unique to this sub-region since the same interaction exists throughout the American West. Aridity, the juxtaposition of ranching and farming with competing interests in water, extractive industries—especially mining—and the exploitation of isolated sites for the disposal of toxic substances all take a toll on the land, its productivity, its beauty, and the integrity of its ecosystems. Because the longer a religious community lives on the land, the more its thought and practice is shaped by the peculiar human difficulties living with aridity and isolation, it is often assumed that Native Americans know better how to handle environmental issues. But this has not proved to be the case. In the face of modern technology, these Native communities also fall into the exploitive practices of the capitalist economy.[15]

Roman Catholicism was superimposed over the Native American bedrock when, with the expansion of the Spanish colonial empire in the Americas, it reached New Mexico and Arizona in the late sixteenth century. While the Roman Catholic religious culture was Spanish, people of Jewish heritage whose families had converted to Christianity under the threat of exile or death were probably among the immigrants who came.[16] It is conceivable, though not documented, that some formerly Muslim *conversos* were also among the Spanish colonists in New Mexico. Despite these possible exceptions, the uniformly Catholic nature of Spanish colonial society is unquestioned.

Moreover, shaped by nearly 700 years of conflict with the Moorish Islamic powers in Spain, it was a militant form of Catholicism that engaged in a perpetual battle with the adherents of what the Spanish regarded as infidel faiths. Forced upon the region as a state church, Catholicism gradually became the religion of the colonial provinces. Parish priests provided stability and endowed the social structures of the society with meaning. The church, which answered to the Spanish crown rather than the Pope or the Vatican hierarchy, cared for the Spanish colonists by keeping the moral order of society, insuring the people's access to the means of their soul's salvation, and furnishing a unified identity to people living a long way from the centers of their civilization.

The Franciscan and Jesuit missionaries who served the mission churches in the Native American communities carried with them the project of creating new citizens for the Spanish empire. Christianization was central to the empire-building project. As citizens of the Spanish empire, the conquored natives needed to be Christian. But the missionaries—located at the margins of native communities—were only able to create a distinctive kind of Catholicism in which Native Americans learned to go to mass, adopted Catholic saints and holy days, but combined the whole with the underlying structures of native religious traditions.

Both the Native and Hispanic religious traditions in Arizona and New Mexico are fundamentally Roman Catholic, but it is a Catholicism never found unmixed with native traditions. Even in those forms of Catholic practice among the newer Mexican immigrants of the twentieth century, Catholic religiosity has native characteristics. The most important of these mixed symbols for the newer Mexican immigration in particular is the Virgin of Guadalupe. Her story originates early in the Spanish colonial period in Mexico, and her appearance at a significant native religious site identified her as a significant Native American expression of the Christian symbol of the Virgin Mary. She has continued for centuries to serve as a point of identity for a people of mixed Spanish and native heritage.

With the success of the Mexican Revolution in the 1820s, Spanish Catholicism became Mexican Catholicism. In Arizona and New Mexico, Spanish-born clergy were expelled and the control of Native American missions, formerly under the control of the Franciscan and Jesuit religious orders, was transferred to the governance of the bishops who placed secular clergy in these isolated parishes. As will be shown, this shift would have implications in the late twentieth century. In the meantime, as long as the legal establishment of the Catholic faith continued, Protestant missionary activity was aggressively discouraged. The right of the state to impose the form of religion was simply taken for granted.

If not Eden, on the surface this sub-region was a thoroughly Catholic world until the conclusion of the Mexican War, at which point the treaty of Guadalupe Hidalgo added Arizona and New Mexico to U.S. territory. Native Americans were everywhere at hand, but in the avenues of influence and power, their presence was negligible. Then Anglos started to arrive. They came in waves, the first of which consisted of merchants and adventurers who desired to profit from trade along the newly opened Sante Fe Trail. If they settled down, they often converted to Catholicism when they married Mexican women, thereby strengthening the area's Catholic character. A second wave of Anglo immigration that began after the Civil War brought a Protestant Christian presence into the Arizona and New Mexico sub-region. Although they established congregations that were part of the historic Protestant mainline, for a long time the Protestant presence was also negligible.

A pervasive anti-foreign atmosphere characterized U.S. culture from the 1840s till well past the First World War. In the eastern part of the nation, this anti-foreign sentiment was particularly directed against the Irish, who were Roman Catholics, and against the post-Civil War "new immigration" that brought Catholics and Jews from European cities to America. The "discovery" that the new territories added to the nation after the Mexican War were heavily Roman Catholic drew the Arizona and New Mexico territories into this general Anglo anxiety over a growing population neither well-versed in Anglo-American cultural values nor in Protestant religious traditions.

As a consequence, Protestant clergy, many of them a part of a strong home missions movement, went to New Mexico and Arizona with two goals: organizing Protestant congregations for the newly arriving Anglo population and converting the Hispanic Roman Catholic population to English-speaking

Protestantism. Unlike the Roman Catholic missionaries who tolerated some mixing of traditions, these Anglo Protestants insisted on keeping a separate identity as they attempted to create a pan-Protestant cultural hegemony. While they initially organized Spanish-speaking churches, they expected that eventually the members would learn to speak English and adopt Anglo cultural forms.

Only the Methodists and Presbyterians had much success during the middle decades of the nineteenth century, and that success was limited. Altogether, the Protestant clergy only managed to convert between 5 and 10 percent of the population to some form of Protestantism. The really significant religious development during these years was the school system the Presbyterians established in New Mexico and Arizona. It rivaled the public school system in size and surpassed it in quality.

With the advent of the Protestant missionaries and their school systems in the 1860s, the Catholic bishop invited the Jesuits, the Christian Brothers, and the Sisters of Loretto to develop a Catholic school system in the Diocese of Sante Fe that included Colorado, as well as Arizona and New Mexico. After that, the religious character of the public school system in New Mexico and Arizona, which did not fully develop until the end of the century, became a source of conflict between Protestants and Catholics. While Protestants throughout the nation conflated Protestantism with Christianity when they spoke of the United States as a Christian nation, they also valued the Constitution and believed that broadly Protestant schools satisfied the non-establishment clause of the Constitution. In this sub-region, the majority of the population was Catholic and the majority of the public school teachers were also Catholic. Creating a broadly Protestant public school system would have been impossible. As a result, so much tension developed in the area of public education that, in 1948, it came to blows, as it were.

Actually, the struggle was not simply about education. When the public school question became a legal issue, it became obvious that the sub-text of the century-long debate about the public schools was that parents who were not Catholic were worried that, in attending public schools, Protestant children were subject to Catholic proselytizing. In Dixon, a small community in the Rio Grande valley between Sante Fe and Taos, Protestant, mostly Presbyterian, parents brought a lawsuit against the local school board on the grounds that the Catholic Church controlled the town's public school.[17] In *Zellers v. Raymond Huff*, Protestants complained that the teachers in Dixon's public school were all Catholic clergy and nuns, and that they imposed Catholic religious practice on all the town's children in the course of their education. A court ruling in 1951 clearly supported the separation of church and state in Dixon and throughout the sub-region.

But the issue of public support for Catholic parochial schools has continued to be an issue of public debate. Its most recent manifestation has been local expressions of concern in which citizens of Arizona and New Mexico have entered into the national controversy over school vouchers that offer parents the opportunity to use state support to send their children to private schools that may or may not be religious. The layers of historical and religious tradition in the sub-region help observers parse the language of debate about school vouchers. The debate takes different parameters in places where communities date from Spanish colonial times than it does where Anglo-Protestants of the mainline traditions in the United States imposed their own understanding of public schools. It differs yet more where Protestants are in the minority or where new immigrant groups fail to recognize the homogenized American civil religion that pertained in classrooms across the country until the 1960s. This is only one example of how highlighting the public policy issues that arise within and between the various cultural layers of Arizona and New Mexico make the religious landscape more visible.

An always visible, but increasingly thick religious layer, particularly in Arizona, is the Mormon layer. The Latter-day Saints early began to extend their range toward both Mexico and California, reaching Arizona by 1878 with settlements in eastern Arizona and the Salt River valley near Mesa and Phoenix. The major early historian of the region, Hubert Howe Bancroft, noted that the Mormon vote was sometimes split according to individual interests but sometimes united on issues of interest to their community in particular. These issues might be general concerns of farmers in an irrigation economy, or more specifically concerns about religious freedom.[18] The strong Mormon opposition to the Equal Rights Amendment in the 1980s, and against any form of gay marriage, indicates that this pattern still holds.

With the advent of the railroad lines and corresponding population increase, African-American immigration also made itself felt late in the post-Civil War era. African Americans settled in the towns having railroad connections because that was a primary source of employment for them. They brought with them their own versions of Protestant traditions, primarily Baptist and Methodist. Both groups, in addition to the Native Americans and Hispanic Catholics, became objects of Anglo Protestant missionary activity.

In the period from 1850 to 1890, public policy issues having religious focus centered on the effort of the Protestant churches to put in place the same kinds of cultural practices they had by and large established in the East: in addition to wanting public schools that would be Protestant in everything but name, they wanted laws enforcing Sabbath keeping. In Arizona and New Mexico, defining the civic calendar of holidays away from the observance of Roman Catholic festivals to those of a broadly Protestant national civil religion became an important issue. The questions of reading the (Protestant) Bible in the public schools, the closure of government offices for Good Friday, and the effort to impose temperance and Sabbath keeping practices by legislation were persistent issues during the period, both in the East and in the West. Almost always, the Catholic majority in Arizona and New Mexico opposed the Protestants on these issues, and as there were more Catholics than Protestants their position often prevailed.

A third wave of Anglo immigration began with the completion of the railroads in the 1880s and continued through the 1920s. This era was characterized by two new Anglo groups made up of a mix of those who came for economic opportunities. Though not the largest, they were certainly the most well known. These were the health seekers and the artists. Before the discovery of antibiotics, the desert climate and high altitudes provided a refuge for those with illnesses as varied as malaria and tuberculosis. These seekers also discovered what were for them exotic healing arts among the Mexicans and Native Americans that promised cures for diseases beyond the reach of contemporary Western medicine.

The same desert landscapes attracted writers and artists. Mary Austin and D. H. Lawrence both stayed and wrote in Taos, using themes derived from the cultural interactions of Native American, Hispanic, and Anglo cultures in that area. The contrast of what they regarded as "civilization" with more "primitive" ways of life intrigued them and they both celebrated and were appalled by the native paganism of the first layers of religion in the region. The Taos group of artists—Ernest Blumenschein, Bert Geer Phillips, Eanger Irving Couse, W. Herbert Dunton, and others—sought to capture the desert and mountain landscape in romantic terms, working with the quality of light, the land forms, and the cultural artifacts. Georgia O'Keeffe found in the bleached bones and bare rocks a way to illustrate the fundamental forces of life and death. Similar communities of artists flourished in Santa Fe, Sedona, and Phoenix.

The arts and crafts of the Pueblo, Navajo, Pima, and Papago peoples also attracted those interested in folk arts. One artist persuaded a Navajo singer and sand painter to create a sacred sand painting in permanent form for artistic display, something many Navajo still regard as sacrilegious. Scholars following the new disciplines of anthropology and archeology found abundant resources for their studies in the Anasazi ruins and the variety of Native American cultures. All of these artists and scholars were in complete disagreement with the established religious authorities, whether they were the ministers of Christian churches or Native religious leaders. They wished to use Native American traditions for artistic and scholarly purposes, and they wanted to preserve them unchanged, keeping them as artifacts rather than as living and therefore constantly changing religious symbols.

A cultural contretemps developed between the artists and scholars on one hand and clerical and missionary leaders on the other. The artists and anthropologists wanted to preserve the Native American cultures unchanged as artifacts for study and as pristine primitive societies, rather like pristine wilderness. On the other hand, the Protestant, Catholic, and Mormon missionaries wanted to completely convert the Native Americans to Christianity, altogether destroying their religious traditions and, hence, their culture. The Protestants and the Mormons were also anxious to convert the Hispanic people away from Catholicism. One means they used for doing this, both with regard to the Native American and Hispanic people, was creating religious schools in which members of their younger generations could be educated as modern Americans (as Protestant or Mormon). Possibly because the missionaries and their clerical leaders realized that wholesale conversion was not likely to occur among adults, most were content to leave the old ways to the elders who would do no harm to practice them for a few more years. Conflict over the public schools included a struggle about whether native children should be removed from their families to be educated in boarding schools, thus being completely separated from their families and their culture. The approaches of both the artist and scholarly communities created unending public conflict within the Native American communities and between them and their intrusive new neighbors.

The discovery of Native American traditions and ancient folk Catholicism by Anglos in the late nineteenth and early twentieth century coincided with an increase in the attraction generated by the notion of spiritual phenomena in general. Interest in the activity of ghosts and spirits, the possibility of communicating with the dead, curiosity about mental healing or psychic influence across a distance, and the discovery of exotic new religions after the World Parliament of Religions in Chicago in 1893, all set the stage for interest in the ancient religious practices Anglos were finding in this newly acquired piece of the United States. As a result, in addition to the health seekers who flocked to the desert, many others found their way to Indian country in Arizona and New Mexico seeking spiritual adventure.

A fourth wave of Anglo immigration started arriving in this sub-region in the 1930s and continued to move into the area during World War II. Consisting initially of distressed inhabitants of the Dust Bowl and Texans and other Southerners who lost their livings and their homes in the Great Depressions, these new immigrants came seeking economic survival. They settled in the cities of Arizona and New Mexico, and some found places in the new farmland created by massive irrigation projects begun in the 1920s and 30s on the Gila and San Juan rivers and the Rio Grande. Religiously they contributed to the "southernization" of the American Southwest. The majority of this wave of newcomers was affiliated with conservative Protestant groups: the Southern Baptist Convention and smaller Baptist groups, Holiness churches (a variety of denominations related to the Methodists who stressed entire sanctification or perfection of life and ranged from mildly conservative to strictly fundamentalist in their theology), and the new Pentecostal churches. From this point forward, the Baptist churches began a steady rise in numbers compared to all other religious groups, and a concerted evangelism effort in the 1950s cemented their hegemony among the Protestant churches in the region. Extending the Bible Belt across southern New Mexico and Arizona, toward Southern California, these new immigrants brought into public religious debates an increasingly conservative Christian voice. In the perennial public school controversies they added the fundamentalist/modernist debates over the teaching of evolution. While they tended to oppose the Catholics on school issues in the early part of the twentieth century, by the end of the century they had often become allies in support of several issues, including school vouchers and family and personal morality.

The fifth and most recent wave of Anglo immigration that began in the 1940s during World War II and continues to the present, could be called the Sunbelt Population Explosion. Particularly affecting Arizona, fueling the huge growth of Phoenix and, to a lesser extent, Tucson and (set in motion by the postwar technology boom) Albuquerque, this phase of Anglo immigration rests on the growth of the technology economy and the migration of retirees out of the Snow Belt to the warmer climates of Florida, New Mexico, Arizona, and Southern California. Phoenix began to be more culturally akin to Southern California than to New Mexico after World War II. Generalizations made about the sub-region of Arizona and New Mexico always must take account of this change.

The growth of the overall population in this period included a rapid expansion in the Jewish and black populations as well as the Anglo population. The economic opportunities in an area relatively less prejudiced than the South had attracted some African Americans during the early twentieth century. Now more came to join them. The many retirees who made this sub-region their home included Jews from northern cities.

In addition, the military and supporting technology economy developing rapidly after World War II attracted a large number of highly educated people. The resulting increasing diversity undercut the magnitude of Hispanic influence, if not the numbers of Hispanics in the population. They remain the largest minority, far surpassing the American Indian population, but both in the old colonial communities and among recent Mexican immigrants, particularly in New Mexico, there is a decline in the use of the Spanish language and declining influence of Hispanic culture, especially in the cities.

Since the 1960s new immigrant communities have entered New Mexico and Arizona in growing numbers. With the changes in the immigration laws, Asian immigrants have been attracted to the area. With them have come additional religious traditions, Islam, Buddhism, Taoism, Hinduism, Sikhism, and their variants. In New Mexico, a sizable Sikh community exists in Española and a mosque calls Muslims to prayer in Abiquiu, both in an area representing the heartland of the older Spanish colonial society and the even older Pueblo cultures. Anglos are being attracted by these new traditions as well. A Hindu ashram in Taos is largely made up of Anglo converts. The Ojo Caliente school system now has to face public policy questions representing old Catholic and Native conflicts, newer Catholic and Protestant conflicts, and now even newer conflicts among at least five of the world's religions.

Finally, since the rise of the New Age movement in the 1960s, which itself was built upon earlier new religious movements and interest in spiritual phenomena, interest in Native American shamanism, geographical locations associated with spiritual energy, and UFOs have flourished in this region, becoming characteristic of it.

Public identity in a culture is shaped by religious definitions of family, enemy, and the location and responsibility of individuals to society. Identity shifts, both as people grow older and as they encounter people from other cultures who offer alternative identities. In this sub-region with its complex religious layers, intermarriage complicates religious identity because it so often unites two separate personas, each with complex religious structures and roots. The public roles people play are complicated when intermarriage brings different religious traditions into proximity in the same family and blurs the distinctions between them.

For centuries Native Americans of different nations or tribes intermarried. During the Spanish colonial period, Spanish settlers married native spouses. Study of the Archdiocese of Santa Fe archives suggests that between 1646 and 1846, slightly more than half of the Pueblo grooms married a Spanish bride, and many Spanish grooms married Pueblo brides.[19] Such marriages mixed Pueblo and Roman Catholic religious traditions, though on the surface they were officially Catholic weddings. These marriages generated public policy concerns in both Pueblo and Hispanic communities over land inheritance and tribal or national citizenship.

In contemporary times intermarriage continues, and it is especially prevalent in the cities where Anglo, Hispanic, and native people blend families and religions regularly. The resulting convoluted kinship structures create public policy issues with religious overtones. Besides the current discussions of the meaning of bi-racial identity, not the least of which is how people are categorized in the census, public policy questions arise about who has access to tribal resources or who counts as an under-represented constituency.

The issue of mixed marriages also complicates the discussions of religious freedom in the region, since the predominant traditions, Christianity and the

Native American religions, are in their own ways exclusive traditions. The former requires assent to certain beliefs, more stringent in more conservative denominations and less stringent in more liberal ones. Even though Christianity has been shaped by syncretism with the religions among which it has lived throughout its history, it always draws a boundary somewhere and says this is Christian and this is not. Native traditions are birthright traditions; only the initiated from within the tribes are invited in. Outsiders are discouraged or forbidden from knowing or practicing the ceremonies that stand at the heart of these traditions. Yet the two kinds of religion have lived side by side for 500 years and syncretism has gone both ways.

The tensions created by the public proximity of separate religious and cultural communities create not only inter-religious conflict, but also tension and conflict within each group. More conservative factions within a community act to preserve the tradition unchanged in order to preserve social order and stability, drawing boundaries and separating their groups as clearly as possible from the others. More liberal factions embrace change, freely borrowing and softening the boundaries between groups, valuing the possibility of something better over a sense of stability and order.

While religion is increasingly considered to be a private matter, with all these new groups and interests, religion remains very much in the public domain. Public policy issues continue to be affected by religion, but not always as they have been in the past. The role of public schools in society, and the degree to which they can be used to foster particular unifying or "religious" ideologies, has taken on new life as conservative Christian groups fight against Harry Potter and celebrating Halloween in the public schools, and for creationism in science textbooks.

Trying to protect sacred ground is no longer simply something Native Americans do. Dave Foreman, the founder of Earth First, who has roots in New Mexico and in the Churches of Christ, preaches a radical gospel in which the political process and human action are sources of evil, while the wilderness and the natural world are deific. His calls for action to preserve the natural world (through tree-sitting, enviro-terrorism, and so on) reflect a system of belief in which salvation is not for individuals but for the planet. The prevalence of military, nuclear, mining, and waste disposal activity in the "uninhabited" desert provokes religious interest, as do more mainline environmental concerns raised by watershed control, irrigation, and limited water supplies.

All these issues are rooted in the history of this sub-region. But nothing in the contemporary religious arena is more imbedded in an often forgotten dimension of the past history of religion in New Mexico and Arizona than the current clerical scandal in the Roman Catholic Church. Back in the 1820s, when Mexico was ridding Catholicism of Spanish influence so that the Roman Church could be a proper state church of what was then a Mexican province, control of mission parishes was removed from the Franciscans and Jesuits and handed over to the secular clergy. Some time afterward, the diocese of Sante Fe was established, placing control of the staffing of all the parishes in New Mexico and Arizona in the hands of a local bishop.

Fast forward to 1992. A "60 Minutes" segment prefigured the Catholic scandal story that erupted in Boston in 2000 with a story about Catholic priests in New Mexico. Bruce Pasternak, an Albuquerque attorney for more than 100 children who claimed to have been abused by 20 priests, told Mike Wallace a horrendous tale. He said: "New Mexico [had] become a center for the accumulation of the world's pedophile priests." A treatment facility operated by a small order of priests known as the "Servants of the Paraclete" that was started in 1947 had, he said, "become the place where pedophiles from all over the world were sent." Paraclete House, as it was called—it is now closed—tried to rehabilitate pedophile priests and, "over the years, many of the priests who came here went to work in the archdiocese of New Mexico when their treatment ended."

In press accounts of Phoenix Bishop Thomas O'Brien's admission of a cover-up of allegations of sex abuse by 50 priests, only one of the involved priests was mentioned as having received treatment in a New Mexico facility before being assigned to a parish in the Phoenix diocese. How many others had similar histories is not known. But Pasternak's "60 Minutes" interview with Mike Wallace, plus O'Brien's admission, strongly suggests that the wide-open spaces of Arizona and New Mexico made this sub-region an ideal place for placing unstable priests with troubled pasts in out-of-the-way parishes where their activities could stay covered up, if not permanently buried.

Overall, the most important religious trends in this sub-region are a gradual increase of Protestant adherents, a decline in the number of Catholic adherents, and a sharp rise in the number of the unaffiliated. The presence of substantial Baptist and Roman Catholic populations keeps New Mexico one of the most "churched" areas in the United States. While Catholics have been a larger proportion of the religiously affiliated up to now, some believe that the Baptists are positioned to rival the Roman Catholics for religious hegemony by 2020.

While the same historic mainline churches that settled Arizona and New Mexico in the years after 1850 remained predominant within Protestantism until the 1990s, United Methodists, Presbyterians, Episcopalians, Congregationalists, and American Baptists are now being edged out by Pentecostal, Holiness, and nondenominational Protestants (mostly new, generally evangelical churches unrelated to existing denominations, but often single, very large congregations with many smaller branches). With these new groups and interests, public policy issues continue to be affected by religion. Some remain the same as they have been in the past. The question of the role of public schools in society, and the degree to which they can be used to foster particular unifying or "religious" ideologies, remains alive. Native Americans continue to experience conflict over their rights to religious sites held by private individuals or governments. The prevalence of military, nuclear, mining, and waste disposal activity in the "uninhabited" desert provokes religious interest as do the environmental concerns raised by watershed control and irrigation, and limited water supplies.

New public policy issues have surfaced related to these perennial concerns. The role of national government agencies like the Park Service in protecting Native American religious sites has been recently debated as the general public with New Age curiosity about holy phenomena desires to see or experience these places. Fundamentalist Christian parents have recently opposed public school celebrations of the Mexican Dia de los Muertos as well as Halloween. The morality of the clergy, not a new issue in any religious tradition, is receiving sustained scrutiny within the Roman Catholic Church, which may not only be affecting the public prestige of that religious institution but also shaking people's faith in religious institutions in general.

Scandal, however, is by no means the whole of the story of Catholicism in this sub-region, much less the whole of the story of religion in this part of the Mountain West. But the ability of bishops in this sub-region to find places for clergy after a course of treatment—whether at Paraclete House or elsewhere—is a reminder that place makes a difference. Urban oases and lightly inhabited spaces form the backdrop for an ongoing religious drama, some part of which— environmental issues, public school matters, clerical scandals—touches everyone in Arizona and New Mexico; even those whose religious identity is "None."

Endnotes

1. *Gracias* to Evelyn Vigil, former editor of the Los Alamos newspaper for several conversations that helped shape this essay.
2. In 1980, in Arizona, 60 percent of the people in the state were not affiliated with any of the religious bodies who reported membership and adherence statistics to the Glenmary Research Center, while, at 41 percent of religiously unaffiliated, the total for New Mexico was 4 percentage points higher than the total percentage reported in 2000. These differences are within reasonable margins of reporting errors.
3. The percentage of the total population in 1990 was 43. But the difference in that percentage and the 43.2 percent in 2000 is too close to be significant because the NARA data have been adjusted to take into account religious organizations that did not report in 2000. As a result, differences of less than a full percentage point are probably statistical aberrations.
4. Bliss Institute data for the Rocky Mountain Region, of which New Mexico and Arizona are a part, must be used with care, because there was a very small sample size for the region.
5. Percentages in County populations.

County	American Indians	Unaffiliated or Uncounted	Members of Religious Bodies
ARIZONA			
Apache	76.9	49.1	50.9
Cocohino	28.5	65.2	34.8
Navaho	47.7	58.3	41.7
NEW MEXICO			
Cibola	40.3	35.3	64.7
McKinley	74.7	59.3	40.8
San Juan	36.9	59.0	41.0

6. In Arizona and New Mexico, Anglo refers to English-speaking Americans, regardless of race.
7. Clearly Tucson and Phoenix are extensions of Los Angeles as a Jewish gathering place in the sense described by Deborah Dash Moore in *To the Golden Cities: Pursuing the American Jewish Dream in Miami and L.A.* (New York: Free Press, 1994).
8. Two works on American religious history emphasize this religious theme of creating a sense of home or belonging in a culture. William Clebsch *American Religious Thought* (Chicago, University of Chicago Press, 1973) argues that theological and philosophical reflection in America, from the English colonial period to the twentieth century, centers on the question of how the newcomer can be at home in a new place, or finally how human beings can be at home in the universe. R. Laurence Moore's *Religious Outsiders and the Making of Americans* argues that Americans seek a sense of identity by casting themselves and their group as outsiders to some (imagined?) mainstream. It is in

the common experience of being outsiders that Americans find themselves at home.

9. Carlos Casteñeda, *The Teachings of Don Juan: A Yaqui Way of Knowledge* (Berkeley: University of California Press, 1998). Reprint.

10. If these sacred sites are located on land that was ceded to various tribes in treaties, Native Americans can bring the issue before the Indian Claims Commission (established in 1946).

11. Evelyn Vigil, who served for several years as a reporter and editor for the Los Alamos newspaper, pointed out the importance of this issue. Practically every week newspapers all across Arizona and New Mexico contain stories about the conflicts arising from contested religious sites.

12. The following paragraph is taken from the Web site of the *Sacred Land Film Project*: "The conflict surrounding 17,000 petroglyphs west of Albuquerque, New Mexico, demonstrates that even a national monument is not safe when it comes to suburban development. A developer and the Albuquerque City Council want to build a six-lane highway through the northern portion of the park to give a new housing development access to the city of Albuquerque. At stake is not just a national monument, but also an area of great spiritual significance: 'The petroglyph area is where messages to the spirit world are communicated. We consider each of these petroglyphs to be a record of visions written here of some spiritual being, event, or expression,' says Bill Weahkee of the Five Sandoval Indian Pueblos, Inc."

13. The *High Country News* is published by the High Country Foundation, a non-profit media organization whose mission is to inform and inspire people to act on behalf of the West's land, air, water, and inhabitants. It works "to create what Wallace Stegner called a society to match the scenery."

14. Both incidents are described in Kathleen Egan Chamberlain's, "Competition for the Native American Soul: The Search for Religious Freedom in Twentieth Century New Mexico," in Ferenc M. Szasz and Richard W. Eutalian eds., *Religion in Modern New Mexico* (Albuquerque: University of New Mexico Press, 1997), 81-100.

15. For a useful discussion of the "Indian Question" in one of the states in this sub-region, see Chamberlain, Ibid.

16. These persons are hard to trace historically because it was illegal for them to practice their faith, causing them to keep their Jewish heritage hidden: See Henry Tobias, *A History of the Jews in New Mexico* (Albuquerque: University of New Mexico Press, 1990).

17. A full description of this case can be found in Janice E. Schuetz, "A Rhetorical Approach to Protestant Evangelism in Twentieth-Century New Mexico," in Szasz and Eutalian, *Religion in Modern New Mexico*, 135-139.

18. Hubert Howe Bancroft, *Arizona and New Mexico, 1530-1888.* (New York: McGraw-Hill, 1967; San Francisco: The History Co., 1889), 534.

19. Ramón Gutiérrez, *When Jesus Came, the Corn Mothers Went Away: Marriage, Sexuality, and Power in New Mexico, 1500-1846* (Stanford, Calif.: Stanford University Press, 1991), 283.

CHAPTER FOUR

THE MORMON CORRIDOR: UTAH AND IDAHO

Kathleen Flake[1]

U tah and Idaho form the core of the Mormon Corridor. Named by cultural
geographer Donald Meinig in 1955, the region's strong religious ethos has
been experienced by all who have lived in the Mountain West since members of
the Church of Jesus Christ of Latter-day Saints (Latter-day Saints or Mormons)
occupied the Great Basin in 1847.[2] Arriving early and colonizing methodically,
the Latter-day Saints and their church have maintained an extraordinarily influential presence throughout the region for more than 150 years. Although North
American Religion Atlas (NARA) data, derived from reports by religious institutions themselves, show that the Mormons constitute only 1.5 percent of the population nationally, descendents of the Mormon pioneers and their converts constitute 14 percent of the population in the Mountain West, nine times the national
average. Within Idaho and Utah, that percentage doubles and quadruples respectively.

Mormon dominance must also be measured in terms of the LDS Church's
economic and political influence. In the nineteenth century, the church created a
communal economy and political theocracy that, notwithstanding modernization,
has left much of the land as well as the commercial and political institutions of this
sub-region of the Mountain West under direct or indirect Mormon control.
Contrary to the experience of founding religions in Massachusetts, Rhode Island,
Pennsylvania, and Virginia, whose social authority and political power were diluted by religious pluralism, the Church of Jesus Christ of Latter-day Saints has
retained both its demographic and cultural dominance in Utah and southern Idaho.

This chapter considers three dimensions of the relation of religion to public
life in the Mountain West. The first dimension is suggested by statistics: a singu-
lar lack of diversity and a single dominant religious institution have created a de
facto religious establishment. The second dimension has to do with the kind of

religion that dominates the region. Mormons are not only intensely self-identified with their church today, but its history and the nature of their faith make them and their church very public actors in all aspects of regional politics and culture.

If Mormonism is very public, however, it is also very private. Consequently, as a belief system, Mormonism gives its adherents a totality of experience and, in exchange, elicits a type of commitment that can isolate them and communicate disrespect to others. In fairness, it should be remembered that America's other religions contributed to Mormon standoffishness by an extended history of attacks upon Mormonism, a uniquely violent exception to the general rule of American religious tolerance. These factors—demographics, theology, and history—combine to make the Great Basin a site of considerable religious tension that often gets played out in the public domain.[3]

The Numbers

The Mormons were the first Europeans to settle in the Great Basin. They came by the thousands and settled in organized communities, not as individual homesteaders. Non-Mormons came as well, but in significant numbers only after 1869, when the driving of a golden spike at Promontory, Utah, signaled completion of the transcontinental railroad. Over the next 15 years, the Mormons' share of the population dropped from 98 to 63 percent. It appears to have settled there.[4] According to NARA, Latter-day Saints make up 66 percent of Utah's population. Catholics come next with 4 percent. All other religious groups each constitute less than 1 percent of the population. Only the religiously unaffiliated, with 23.5 percent, can claim double-digit representation.

The nature of religion in the Great Basin challenges the category "religiously unaffiliated" as generally applied by NARA. Many of the unaffiliated may be lapsed Mormons who do not worship with "the Saints" but continue to be motivated by the church's worldview or have some loyalty to its traditions. In Utah and Idaho's historically Mormon towns, disinterest in organized religion can mask a visceral attachment to several generations of pioneers and missionaries and an inheritance of their habits, if not their devotion. When, for example, 47 percent of the 921 residents of Utah's Daggett County claim to be religiously unaffiliated, but all the others espouse Mormonism, diversity may not run very deep. Mormonism's uncontested dominance over the region does not rely on such subtleties, however. In 26 of Utah's 29 counties, Mormons constitute a raw majority of the general population. In 10 of those counties, the Mormon majority is 80 percent or higher.

Idaho's demographics show more diversity than Utah's, but still are marked by Mormonism. The state is comprised of three geographic and cultural sections, in terms of its non-indigenous populations.[5] Its agricultural land to the south is an extension of the Great Basin and, especially in the southeast, was colonized in the 1870s at the direction of Brigham Young. These counties have a robust Mormon population, constituting between 35 and 92 percent of the area's residents and retain a social and cultural orientation to Salt Lake City. Idaho's southwestern counties gravitate naturally to its capital city, Boise, and are home to the state's major corporate interests, as well as federal military and regulatory agencies. Depending upon how the counties are apportioned between these two areas, Mormon concentration in southwest Idaho averages 15 percent, compared to 61 percent in the southeast.[6]

Idaho's northern panhandle is divided from the south by Hell's Canyon, the deepest gorge in North America. This rugged terrain was settled in the 1860s by miners, but fur traders and Jesuits had preceded them by 20 years. The latter established Catholicism among the Coeur d'Alenes. Their Cataldo Mission, built in 1853, was the first church in Idaho and remains today the state's oldest building. Many of the miners who later came into the region were of Irish descent, adding to early predominance of Catholicism in the north. Such cultural divisions between Idaho's north and south were maintained by Hell's Canyon, which inhibited the flow of commerce and traffic until the late twentieth century and even today requires a detour outside the state's boundaries when traversing the state. Over time, northern Idaho's natural tie with the terrain and peoples to its west has caused a greater identity with them than with Idahoans to the south.

Like their Pacific Coast neighbors, the panhandle counties have a high number of religiously unaffiliated; in some cases higher than Oregon's 65 and Washington's 62 percent averages. Consequently, the north displays today greater religious diversity than the south. In most counties, the population is fairly evenly balanced among Catholics, Mormons, evangelicals, and the historic mainline Protestants, with a small representation of non-Christian adherents. For instance, of the 37 percent of Latah County's residents who are religious, 8 percent are Catholic; 8 percent are Mormon; 4 percent are Holiness or Pentecostal; 4 percent are Lutheran; 3 percent are conservative Christians; 2 percent are Baptist; 2 percent are Methodist; 2 percent are Presbyterian; 2 percent are Muslim; and the remainder (at less than 1 percent each) are Episcopalian, Christian Church (Disciples), mainline liberal Christians, Jews, and adherents of Eastern religions. In a few areas, however, Catholics have retained their historic majority, such as in Idaho County, where they constitute almost half of all religious adherents and 18 percent of the population at large.

Finally, Northern Idaho's geographic isolation appears to have encouraged religious independence as well. The state is famous for providing cover for quasi-religious movements seeking absolute freedom from the law. Nearly a quarter of the religious adherents in Adams and Bonner Counties are conservative

Christians. In addition, radical groups like the Nazi-inspired Church of Jesus Christ Christian and World Aryan Congress at Hayden Lake have been drawn to the remoteness of Idaho's northern counties. The high incidence of unaffiliated in the northern counties, coupled with the great variety of churches, gives no religious group an identifiably dominant role in local public life. As a result, statewide, then, the Mormons remain the largest proportion of Idaho's population with 24 percent, while Catholics follow at 10 percent. This, of course, has political ramifications.

In terms of its capacity to mobilize that portion of the population with religious commitments in the Utah-Idaho sub-region, the LDS Church can assume that more than 80 percent of Utah's and almost 50 percent of Idaho's religious adherents identify with Mormonism at some level. Only three of Utah's 29 counties are less than 70 percent Mormon; four are 99.5 percent or higher.[7] Even in Utah's more metropolitan areas, the church claims 80 percent of the total number of religious adherents. Thus, contrary to the general rule, Utah's population centers are not the most secular or the most religiously diverse.

In Salt Lake City, site of the state's capital and also LDS Church headquarters, the population within the metropolitan boundaries is about evenly divided between Mormon and non-Mormon. But the surrounding suburbs in Salt Lake County are mostly Mormon. Only 30 percent of the county's population claims to be unaffiliated, itself an extraordinary figure for a metropolitan area of approximately 900,000 people. It is also remarkably homogeneous: Mormons constitute 80 percent of all the county's adherents; the remaining 20 percent is split among many faith communities that achieve a measure of numerical significance only when grouped in broad historical or theological categories: Roman Catholics and Orthodox Christians together constitute 9.2 percent; Protestants 5.8; Eastern religions 1.7; Jews .7; and Muslims .6 percent. No single Protestant church has numbers in excess of 1 percent in Salt Lake City or even statewide.

Diversity Not

If the amount of religion in the Mormon Corridor is the first conclusion drawn from the NARA, the second is its homogeneity. Considering that the nation is famous for its religious diversity, the nearly absurd lack of such diversity in Utah's makeup is revealed by the kind of questions provoked by the NARA data. Why, for instance, are only (not "as many as") 59 percent of Grand County's religious adherents Latter-day Saints? The answer appears to lie in a combination of radical terrain and Native American resistance that stymied Mormon settlement intentions until the late 1870s. In addition, mining became the area's chief industry at a time when church authorities discouraged it among members.

Not until 1937 did the area achieve sufficient population to be granted status as a separate county. Today, the steep canyons of the Colorado River that served to hide Butch Cassidy and the Sundance Kid are national parks and nationally famous recreational venues, including the city of Moab, mecca to four-wheel drive enthusiasts. Grand County's residents, while still 3 percent above the regional average of 48 percent, are only half as religious as their fellow Utahns. Next to the Church of Jesus Christ of Latter-day Saints, the Baptists claim the most members with 20 percent of the county's religious adherents; all other Protestants combined come in third, with 11 percent; with Catholics close behind, at 10 percent.

The other two Utah counties where less than 70 percent of religious adherents are Mormon tell a similar story. Summit County, once famous for its Park City silver mines, is today a skiers' paradise with its own brewery. Nevertheless, as a gateway from the east through the Wasatch Mountains to the Salt Lake Valley, the region retains a Mormon ethos. Only 40 percent of its residents are not unaffiliated or uncounted; 62 percent of all church adherents are Latter-day Saints. With 67 percent Mormon affiliation, Carbon County, too, has its history in the mining industry and, like Summit, 18 percent of its religious affiliates are Catholic. Federal geologist Marcus E. Jones was right in 1890 when he reported to the U.S. Treasurer: "Had ores not been easily smelted, Utah would still be Mormon only."[8]

In Idaho, members of the Church of Jesus Christ of Latter-day Saints constitute 70 percent or more of adherents in 14 of 44 counties and between 40 and 65 percent of another five counties. These counties are in the more densely populated southern end of Idaho, and suggest greater political leverage than the numbers alone communicate. For example, in Ada County, home of Boise, the state capital (one of the state's three counties with a population greater than 100,000), 32 percent of the religious adherents are Latter-day Saints. Catholics are the second most numerous, with 26 percent; and conservative Protestants are third, at 11 percent. In Canyon County, after Ada the state's second most populous county, 33 percent of the religious adherents are Latter-day Saints.[9]

Latter-day Saint adherents constitute the majority of all adherents in the state's three counties with populations between 50,000 and 100,000. In Bannock and Bonneville counties, of all adherents they are 75 and 70 percent respectively. In Bonneville, the Saints outnumber all other adherent categories combined, including the unaffiliated or uncounted. In Twin Falls County, Latter-day Saints constitute 38 percent of adherents; Catholics follow at 17 percent; and Holiness/Wesleyan, combined with Pentecostals, constitute 10 percent. Finally, in three of the seven counties with cities with populations between 20,000 and 50,000, Latter-day Saints have majorities ranging from 66 to 99 percent.

This means that Mormon dominance in the Great Basin is so disproportionately high that it is difficult to give an account of other religions in an essay devoted to religion's public role. In Utah County, for example, home of Brigham Young University and a population of approximately 370,000, of whom 88 percent are Mormon, what effect can the roughly 370 Baptist or even 3,700 Catholic residents have on local government? How does their voice register in school board meetings or on local tax initiatives? Given, however, the affinity of Mormons, Baptists, and Catholics on certain social questions, such as same-sex unions and abortion, one might as easily worry about the 1,100 unaffiliated who constitute only 9 percent of the population.

The political consequences of Mormon dominance are most easily measured on the national and state level, however. In terms of political office, all the members of Utah's Congressional delegation except one are both Mormon and Republican. The lone Democrat is not an active member of the LDS Church, but his constituents regard him as a "cultural Mormon." The state has not had a non-Mormon governor since 1957. Presently, four of five justices of the state supreme court and 90 percent of its legislature are Latter-day Saints. While each of these public servants may be as independent-minded as any other religious person, it remains a fact that there are few such "other religious persons" among Utah's political leaders. Even if the state's officialdom self-consciously seeks independence from their religious ideology while on the job, the point is that Utah's homogeneity requires such self-consciousness because the social system itself lacks diversity of religious perspective.

The situation in Idaho likewise reflects the state's religious demographics. The state-published *Blue Book for 2001-2002* reveals that 30 percent of Idaho's Senate and 34 percent of its House were then Latter-day Saints, slightly higher than the church's 24 percent portion of the state's population. At the national level, Latter-day Saints occupy half of the state's two Senate and two House seats. The concentration of the Mormon population in the state's Second Congressional District (Southeastern Idaho) almost guarantees that at least one House seat will be held by a member of the LDS Church.[10]

Not only its numerical strength, but also its stance on the issues, appear to make Mormon political activity obvious to others in this Mountain West subregion. In an interview for this chapter, an expert in Idaho politics said that he believed he could tell which legislators are Latter-day Saints by the conservative nature of their voting records. Regardless of the accuracy of his assumption, it appears to be widely shared. According to Gregory Hahn's report in the *Idaho Statesman* of June 19, 2000, the loss of Pocatello, "one of the few Idaho cities to offer genuine two-party debates," to the Republicans is credited in part to the rising numbers of Latter-day Saints in Bannock County.

Utah is so famously and conservatively homogeneous that neither party puts much effort into presidential campaigning there, one party believing it does no good and the other confident it is not necessary.

Research data confirm that the LDS Church is the most single-party religious institution in the nation. The American Religious Identification Study (ARIS) provides information about the way people in the United States identify themselves religiously and politically. ARIS data for 2001 reveal that, while the Latter-day Saints' 55 percent affiliation with the Republican Party is equal to that of evangelical fundamentalists, fewer Mormons deem themselves either independents or members of some party other than the two major parties.

In the last decade of the twentieth century, the LDS Church became concerned about the lopsided political situation in the Mormon culture region. Marlin K. Jensen, a high-ranking church official, was assigned to speak publicly on the proposition that one can be a Democrat and a good Mormon. As reported in an interview with the *Salt Lake Tribune* on April 3, 1998, he said, "We are [concerned] locally and I think there is a feeling that even nationally as a church, it's not in our best interest to be known as a one-party church. The national fortunes of the parties ebb and flow." Since then, during election season, letters from church headquarters not only encourage local congregations to be politically active, but also newly emphasize the importance of a two-party system.

The Church of Jesus Christ of Latter-day Saints is, however, a presence in politics not only indirectly through its members but also directly through its leadership. Each year in Utah, representatives of the state legislature meet formally with high-ranking church officials who are assigned to monitor political issues. "Before every general session, leadership from both parties are invited down to meet with the church's Special Affairs Committee," Utah's speaker of the House told a *Salt Lake Tribune* reporter on January 6, 2002. He added, "We've done that for as long as I've been up here."

Utah's congressional delegation is no less responsive. A prime example is the church's opposition in the early 1980s to a federal proposal to place an intercontinental missile system in Beaver County, Utah. The church's First Presidency issued a formal statement that the MX missiles were not welcome in the state, causing a reversal in position by Utah's then-powerful Senator Jake Garn and contributing materially to the demise of the project. Evidently, the thought of 200 ballistic missiles circulating on a track among 4,200 shelters did not comport with the church's concept of Zion.

More commonly, the LDS Church uses its political influence to protect its ecclesiastical programs, economic interests, and moral order. This includes a wide variety of regulatory issues, from the regulation of water rights locally to national tax policy. Moreover, the extent of the church's economic holdings and, in Utah, its proprietary sense that the sub-region is its homeland, broaden the church's political interests to include a surprising range of otherwise secular issues, even ballistic missiles. The church attracts most attention, however, for its influence on issues it deems moral, such as alcohol consumption, women's rights, and same-sex unions.

Mormons abstain strictly from alcohol and Utah regulates its sale just as strictly. The causative relationship between these two facts is no secret. On February 3, 2003, according to the *Salt Lake Tribune*, church authorities and the Utah Department of Alcoholic Beverage Control (DABC) commissioners met to discuss impending changes to the state's liquor laws. In response to a federal court's rejection of Utah's broad restraints on liquor advertising, including pro-scriptions against asking a customer if he or she wanted a drink or a wine list, local regulators had proposed changes to other elements of the law as well.

The new regulations allowed Utah's drinkers to have two glasses in front of them at dinner and to take an unfinished bottle home. They could also be offered flights of wine, as long they did not exceed five ounces. Beer, however, remained a diluted 3.2 percent and, while more restaurants would have access to liquor licenses (though at a higher price), bars were still required to function as private clubs and were newly required to serve food on the premises. To the predominate-ly Mormon DABC, the new rules were "a product of seeking public comment." To restaurant owners who did not perceive themselves to be a part of the public whose "comments" mattered, the new laws "reflect the culture of the state. And the culture of this state is a dominant religion."

As might be expected, the less dominant position of the church in Idaho has affected the application of Latter-day Saint mores onto the broader population. Specifically, while Utah has repeatedly rejected a state lottery, gambling was legalized in 1989 in Idaho, but only after LDS Church leaders made a determined effort in opposition. In an unusual display of ecclesiastical force, a member of the church's ruling council who was also a former Utah Supreme Court justice was dispatched to Idaho to speak publicly against the state's lottery initiative with a sermon on the "Evils of Gambling." In response to his exhortation, local ecclesi-astical leaders also spoke against the measure, instructing the people in their wards (congregations) to vote against the lottery and asking them to encourage their neighbors to do the same. Their efforts failed, however, suggesting that on issues where individual conscience is concerned, the advice of LDS leadership may have less impact than is sometimes supposed. Nevertheless, both Utah's reli-giously identifiable regulatory law and Idaho's resistance to it signify not only that religion matters in the Great Basin, but also that "a" specific religion matters. Thus, the nature of Mormonism is as important as its numbers are to understand-ing the effect of religion on public life in the Great Basin.

The Nature of the Great Basin's Religions: Minority and Majority

In theological terms, Latter-day Saints have historically understood God as essentially related to the world and themselves as employed in the work of preparing the world for the millennial reign when the heavenly and earthly kingdoms of God would be joined. Until then, the two spheres—the earthly temporal and the heavenly spiritual—would work in concert to accomplish this goal. Believers generally preferred the metaphor of kingdom to that of ecclesia. It conveyed the scope of their project to live in a place, not just within an assembly, governed by the law of God and possessing the power to bind or give efficacy to their earthly works and associations in the heavenly kingdom as well.[11] Not unlike the traditional Catholic notion of the "communion of Saints," the Latter-day Saints believed that the earthly church participated in both eternal and temporal worlds. Three principles were derived from this fusion of the ideal and the real:

- First, there was properly no distinction between the temporal and spiritual government of the Latter-day Saints.
- Second, temporal property and labor were to be dedicated to spiritual purposes, including the good of the collective body of Saints and the building up of the Kingdom of God on the earth.
- Third, covenants made between individuals and consecrated by church ordinance were not temporal, but eternal.

The Mormons left U.S. territorial boundaries because the extremity of the differences between them and Protestant America made coexistence impossible. Successive conflicts with their neighbors in New York, Ohio, Missouri, and Illinois convinced the Saints that "liberty in a solitary place and in a desert is far more preferable than martyrdom in these pious states."[12] The Great Basin provided the desired solitude. By the 1860s, thanks to geographical distance and the nation's preoccupation with the southern insurrection, the Latter-day Saints had successfully constructed political, economic, and familial structures in the West that actualized their highest theology and governed their everyday lives.

The nineteenth-century Mormon settlements in the Mountain West region constituted a complex, unified, and fully developed society established outside of and in contrast to the rest of antebellum America. It consisted of a communal economic system that conscientiously rejected capitalism; a political system that mirrored the Mormon ecclesiastical structure; and a polygamous family system. These interlocking systems that brought all of life under the aegis of the church were displayed to the outside world when, in making the first of several failed attempts for statehood in 1849, the Mormons proposed a government comprised exclusively of the ranking ecclesiastical officers of their church.

The Mormons' economic unity was, like their political unity, seen as an attempt to unlawfully control individual freedom, especially that of non-Mormons. When the discovery of local mineral deposits and the completion of the intercontinental railroad threatened to make the Mormons dependent on eastern manufactured goods and a cash economy, Mormon leadership initiated a cooperative movement that encouraged self sufficiency through home industry and discouraged Mormons from trading with the Gentiles, as all non-Mormons were called. Concerns about Mormon exclusionary and anti-capitalist efforts were, however, outweighed by fear of the economic might of the church itself. As early as the Morrill Act of 1862, the opening salvo in anti-polygamy legislation, Congress attempted to limit the amount of real estate the church could hold to $50,000, requiring forfeiture of excess amounts. The explicit goal was preventing the accumulation of wealth by "theocratic institutions inconsistent with our forms of government."[13]

Although each of these categories of difference has changed sufficiently to permit the inclusion of Mormonism into America's religious body politic, the ideological biases of each remain in the twenty-first century Church of Jesus Christ of Latter-day Saints and help explain many of its public choices, as well as the reaction of its neighbors.

The political dimension of Mormonism—its conflation of the temporal and the eternal—has always been a source of concern for its fellow citizens. In Missouri, fears of Mormon cohesive voting power were a precipitating factor in the church's violent expulsion from that state. Antagonism to the Mormon vote was not based solely in its homogeneity; it was grounded also in America's fundamental objection to a priestly organization that culminates in a prophet-president. Even though the church's priesthood was "of all believers," it was a much more sacramental system than that embraced by Protestantism and, more problematically, was led by one who claimed to speak for God.

As such, Mormonism's ecclesiastical order was believed to inhibit the free exercise of conscience and, thus, undermine the morality necessary to sustain democracy. To Protestants, Mormonism was a "Romanish" or "popish" threat to republican government. To all of America, Mormonism's belief in modern revelation and new scripture made Latter-day Saints antinomian to a rare degree, even in a nation characterized by its religious enthusiasm.

More to the point, the Latter-day Saints' devotion to a law-giving prophet gave them the potential to be a law unto themselves. Fears of theocracy were exacerbated by the territory's petition for statehood that conflated political and ecclesiastical office. Church leaders at all levels were not only pastors of flocks, but also priestly administrators of an earthly kingdom. Thus, the Mormon Zion was not merely a religious ideal, but a completely realized city-state laying between the Great Plains and the California gold fields—a full-blown theocracy in the heart of a would-be enlightened republic.

As strange as it sounds today, Utah's religious establishment was permissible under nineteenth-century constitutional law that had not yet imposed First Amendment restraints on the states. Only the federal government was prohibited from establishing a religion. Unfortunately for Latter-day Saints, however, their legal argument was overtaken by a limitation of states rights by civil war and a judicially enforced ideology of national identity and reform. In the final two decades of the nineteenth century, the church with the soul of a nation and the nation with the soul of a church negotiated which parts of the Mormon Kingdom had to be reconfigured in order for Great Basin residents to join the United States. Eventually, a compromise between Mormons and the nation required the subordination of church marital law to federal law. But much of the church's ideological framework and actual power over Great Basin politics and economics, as well as Mormon social cohesion in the form of family tribalism, was left intact.

Renunciation of polygamy was the chief price the church paid for its acceptance within the nation's religious polity. One cannot, today, be polygamous and a member of the LDS Church; excommunication is immediate for those who try. Indeed, for contemporary Mormons, the practice is so unacceptable that inquiries concerning it are often experienced as one of those "have you stopped beating your wife" questions, asked with an apparent resistance to any answer but what is already assumed. For example, some news analysis in the Elizabeth Smart kidnapping sought to explain her trance-like response to her polygamous captors in terms of the LDS Church former practices. For Latter-day Saints, such explanations echoed old prejudices about the morality of Mormon marriage and charges of an evil mesmerism to explain its practice.

If continuity exists between earlier and contemporary church marriage practice, it is found in the continuing Mormon conviction that marriage has salvific potential and functions to create familial bonds of eternal significance. Such ideology underlies the LDS Church's public fight against recent initiatives to broaden the definition of marriage to include same-sex unions. The irony of the LDS Church's battle to preserve a particular model of marriage at the expense of another is too obvious not to reveal the extent of contemporary Mormonism's alienation from its past. Indeed, as the current church president tells it:

> People mistakenly assume that this Church has something to do with
> that [contemporary polygamy]. It has nothing whatever to do with it.
> It has had nothing to do with it for a very long time. It's outside the
> realm of our responsibility. These people are not members.[14]

It can also be argued, however, that "plural marriage," as the Latter-day

Saints denominated their family system, remains a dimension of their sacred cosmology and supports their deeply felt sense of difference from the broader culture. But neither of these residuals motivate the church to defend polygamy or prevent the church from applying its own theologically based morality to justify intervention in present legislative debates about lawful forms of marriage and sexual conduct. Idaho and Utah were the only states in the Mountain West region with anti-sodomy statutes before the Supreme Court struck down those laws in June 2003.

The LDS theology of marriage can also drive a wedge between Mormons and their neighbors. A news poll published June 27, 2002 by the *Logan Herald Journal*, a newspaper serving a university population not far from the Idaho border, found that "70 percent of church members would object to their children marrying outside of the faith." Only 8 percent of all others polled felt this way. Obviously, since opposition to marriage outside the faith dramatically affects their social relations, this is one of the factors making Mormons appear exclusive.

Just as problematic in a pluralistic culture is the amount of time Latter-day Saints devote to their church callings. On the congregational and diocesan level, church positions are all filled by laity, including positions that paid clergy fill in other churches. Coupled with a three-hour Sunday meeting schedule and temple attendance requirements, these commitments remove Mormons from the ordinary stream of non-Mormon social activity. For those who do not understand the theological basis for these phenomena, Mormons appear at best only superficially involved with those not of their faith and, at worst, elitist by a maddeningly self-referential standard of what is worthy.

Politically, the story is equally complicated. On one hand, the LDS Church has clearly removed all formal ties between ecclesiastical and political office. As the sociologist Thomas O'Dea observed many years ago, the fact that political trends in Utah are largely consistent with the nation as a whole indicates that the church does not absolutely control politics in the Great Basin. "In fact," O'Dea said, "while exerting political influence, the church leadership often points with pride to the fact that it does not control the vote, an interesting reaction conditioned by generations of gentile resentment and suspicion on this score."[15] Years of faith-based political battles have sensitized the Church of Jesus Christ of Latter-day Saints to its critics' claims and, as O'Dea noted, made it useful for the church to lose on occasion. Nevertheless, there are theological limits to how far the LDS leadership is willing to go in remaining politically neutral.

In particular, though the theocratic apparatus has been thoroughly dismantled, accepting the church's prophet-president's jurisdiction over temporal and spiritual matters remains a part of the Mormon faith. While some members may resent church direction in political matters deemed moral and may exercise their agency to disagree with a given political position of the church's leadership, public dissenters are remarkably few. To disagree publicly becomes an issue of faith and can result in separation from the body of the church. Indeed, tension between hierarchically defined positions and contrary ones espoused by individual Mormons is a significant part of the public expression of religion in the Great Basin, most especially in Utah's Salt Lake County. Nationally, this tension has also been apparent—most recently in the church's campaign against same-sex unions and, most effectively, in its campaign against the ERA.[16]

Thus, while the LDS Church takes great pains not to endorse candidates or engage in party politics, it does not hesitate to take a position on political issues it deems threatening to its worldview. When it does act politically on specific local initiatives—alcohol and gambling, for example—the church offends keen sensibilities about church-state separation, if only because the church is so often determinative of the outcome. A local brewer voiced his displeasure with Utah's new liquor laws by marketing a new label, "First Amendment Lager," with the slogan "Taxation without Representation is Utah."

Finally, although the economic commonwealth that was the Utah Territory became a capitalist market with statehood, the idea that the hierarchically organized church acts on behalf of its members temporally, not just spiritually, remains a part of Mormonism's basic ideology. In his history of Mormonism's nineteenth-century, *Great Basin Kingdom*, Leonard Arrington said it best:

> The church's prime obligation was to forward the building of the Kingdom, and that meant it had positive functions to perform in increasing the production of goods and services. In line with this basic orientation, church funds were used to promote many types of new enterprises, ecclesiastical officials regulated many phases of economic activity.[17]

Today, as well, church leadership continues to actively maintain its traditional property interests, developing commercial business opportunities in service to "the building of the Kingdom."

Because information about the church's financial holdings is not public, it is impossible to know with certainty the extent of the church's economic power in the Mountain West. Those who have attempted to quantify it are forced to generalize. In the 1980s, one study pointed to church ownership of "the 13 radio and TV stations, the four insurance companies, the hotel, the newspaper, the big farms . . . the real estate companies (which control four square blocks of prime real estate in the center of Salt Lake City), the clothing mills, the book company, all the schools, the welfare farms and industries, the big department store downtown, [and] the investment portfolio."[18]

Since this list was compiled, both the church and its host economy have boomed. The *Salt Lake Tribune* estimated the church's assets as "exceeding $20 billion" in a December 9, 2001 news story. Even if conservative estimates of church assets, such as that by the *Economist* in February 2002, of $6 billion are closer to the truth, the church's total income from tithes and investments, combined with the value of its tangible property, make it comparable to the region's largest corporations in income generation and numbers of employees. Thus, like its numbers in the Mormon Corridor, the church's economic power also is growing. Inexorably, these developments contribute to the church's political position.

In sum, the Church of Jesus Christ of Latter-day Saints' dominating presence in the Great Basin is naturally part of the region's history. But it is equally a function of the church's theology of time and place. The church's raison d'etre is to sanctify the temporal and prepare it to meet the eternal in time, even a second time when Christ comes again. This requires an assertive engagement in temporal affairs that will build God's kingdom on earth and throughout the earth. The internationalization of the church has not, however, diminished Mormon attachment to the region as its heartland. America's Great Basin remains the Mormons' "right place," as Brigham Young pronounced it upon his arrival in the valley of the Great Salt Lake.

Mormons consider it their rightful place as well. Having figured out how to sustain life in its deserts, they appear intent on hanging on to the fruits of their sacrifice. Moreover, they appear intent on retaining their historic cultural dominance over the sub-region, keeping it the concrete expression of their world view and a haven for the deployment of their ecclesiastical mission throughout the world. For the Mormons, the Mormon Corridor is a homeland, not just the site of church headquarters. Its pioneer temples and cemeteries constitute sacred space and the church will expend every effort to preserve it as such. Nowhere is this more apparent than in the recent crisis over what do with a one-block segment of Salt Lake City's Main Street.

In 1998, city administrators and the LDS Church presidency announced that the portion of Main Street that runs between Mormonism's Temple Square and church headquarters would be sold to the church for $8.1 million. Consistent with the city's "Second Century Plan," the church planned to use the property for a park-like plaza that would join the two tourist centers that attract 9 million visitors each year. While pedestrians would have access through the plaza, control was ceded to the church, allowing it to forbid smoking, sunbathing, bicycling, obscene or vulgar speech, dress, or conduct, and preaching or proselytizing it did not endorse.

To its critics, the plan was a conspiratorial land grab by a church that had run roughshod over local interests to enhance its already too-public presence and to silence dissent in the area adjacent to its religious landmarks. Supporters responded that the sale was merely the last piece of a 40-year master plan to revitalize downtown, the result of a long public process initiated by civic leaders that would inure to the city's financial benefit. Moreover, the church itself argued, the restrictions on public liberty were consistent with traditional principles of private ownership, as well as dictated by the existing religious nature of the two church properties joined by the new plaza.

The traditional parties stepped forward to test the arrangement. With help from the ACLU, the First Unitarian Church of Salt Lake City (which objected to provisions limiting proselytizing to Mormons), Utahans for Fairness (who protested the church's stand on gay rights), and the Utah chapter of NOW (who had fought church politics in the ERA campaign) joined to ask the federal courts to nullify the contract's restraints on use and speech. After losing in federal distict court, an appellate court found that the contract's retention of an easement for pedestrian use created public, not sacred space.

Therefore, it was held that plaza restraints on speech had to pass constitutional muster. On October 10, 2002, the Rev. Tom Goldsmith of the First Unitarian Church responded to his victory by telling the *Deseret News* that the lawsuit "had to happen . . . It's about time we leveled the playing field in hearing a diversity of speech and opinion." Sports metaphors do not do justice to the level of conflict galvanized by the plaza dispute, nor the local powers brought to bear on its solution.

As the furor over the sale appeared to gather public support, the church distributed to the media and to Salt Lake's business, civic, and religious leaders a sophisticated brochure explaining its legal position. A portion of the brochure listed a few recent financial contributions by the church to the city's infrastructure, including land for the city's convention center and concert hall, leased from the church for $1 per year; "sustaining support" for Utah's symphony, ballet, and opera; significant cash and labor donated for construction and restoration of local Catholic, Greek Orthodox, and Presbyterian churches; and $800,000 for a municipal mass transit study. In addition, the church noted that it had given $5 million to the Salt Lake Olympic Committee and provided a block of downtown real estate for the Olympic Medals Plaza.

Though not complete, or even a sufficient measure for the purpose of generalizing about the church's domain, this brochure provided a rare glimpse of the LDS Church's public role in the state's capital city. It was intended, no doubt, to assure the local population that the church was a good, even benevolent, corporate citizen that could be trusted to manage the plaza in the city's best interest. But the list evidenced also the church's controlling position within the community and even constituted a reminder that Salt Lake's citizens were beholden to the church for much of what made their city work. The brochure was by no means a threat, but it was a display of force.

In the end, Rev. Goldsmith's victory was short-lived. While the matter was on appeal to the Supreme Court, tension on the plaza escalated. Two weeks after the Court of Appeals restored "diversity of speech and opinion," the *Salt Lake Tribune* reported in "Day of Heckling on Plaza" that one protestor shouted to a group of 12-year-old Mormon girls: "I'd rather be a homosexual than fornicate with you." In December, a local TV station showed evangelical missionaries passing out anti-Mormon literature and shouting through bullhorns at wedding parties posing on Temple Square. Photos in the January papers showed demonstrators bearing placards with anti-Mormon slogans, such as "Jesus Saves; Joseph [Smith] Enslaves."

Such reports caused even the mayor, a former ACLU attorney and avowed secularist, to reverse course. He abandoned a plan to try to impose constitutional limits on church regulation of the space and agreed to sell the easement itself to the church. On June 23, 2003, the same day as the Supreme Court declined to hear the church's appeal, Salt Lake's City Council approved the mayor's plan. In exchange for the easement, the city received church-owned land for a new community center as well as money to build it from several people affiliated with the church.

The Associated Press report of that same date, headlined "Free Speech, Religion Collide on SLC Plaza," concluded that "the dispute widened a chasm that exists between the city's dominant Mormon population, and non-Mormons who complain of being forced to live by the church's precepts." Hearing such complaints, non-residents tended to agree with a 2002 *Economist* reporter who said, "these charges are exaggerated. The alcohol laws [for example] are annoying rather than oppressive." And, it is true that the amount of regulation and even the objects of regulation in Utah have much in common with other areas of the country. The South's conservative Protestantism has strictly regulated alcohol sales and consumption for years. Kentucky still has more dry counties than wet ones.

But the experience of public religion in the Great Basin is greater than the sum of its regulatory parts. The reported "chasm" between the sub-region's Mormon and non-Mormon residents is the result of 150 years of minority experience by those who elsewhere are the majority. This enduring experience of religious difference and reversal of cultural authority is an important dynamic in the Mormon Corridor. While each of the Mormon Corridor's religions has a uniquely valuable story of sacrifice and hope, travail and triumph in this far western frontier, the role of non-Mormon religion in a narrative of the public role of religion in the Great Basin is largely that of opposition.

The great distance between first and second and the existence of no statistically significant third religious community has polarized religious sentiment in this sub-region of the Mountain West. It has caused some among the non-Mormon population to hold their religious identity more tightly. It has also caused them to forget their differences with other non-Mormon religions and the unaffiliated in order to gain some measure of collective strength in the Mormon Corridor. Thus, the statistical gap between Mormon numbers and those of all other religions becomes an important part of the story of religion in the Mormon Corridor.

The Gap

While it is common to assume that churches over-report their membership and adherent numbers, this appears not to be the case with the Church of Jesus Christ of Latter-day Saints. ARIS data, based on self-reports by individuals, consistently report higher numbers of Mormons in all regions than the institutionally based NARA data report. Specifically, NARA calculates Mormon representation among all Mountain religious adherents to be 27 percent, but ARIS data show Mormon self-identifcation at 47 percent. By contrast, NARA data put Catholic affiliation at 34 percent, but ARIS data shows the percent of self-reported Catholics to be 15 percent. In short, more people consider themselves affiliated to the LDS Church than are recognized on formal records of membership.

Whatever this means for the definition of what it is to be a Mormon, for our purposes it means that the NARA numbers are probably too conservative in their description of LDS adherence at 87 and 48 percent in Utah and Idaho, respectively. NARA data also suggests that the gap between Mormon and Catholic representation, as great as it is, may even be greater, if the extent of Catholic self identification is as low as calculated by ARIS. Of the 12 Idaho counties where NARA data show more Catholics than Mormons, ARIS reverses six and causes the difference in three more to become statistically insignificant. This continuing gap in numbers is paralleled historically by a gap in resources and interfaith affection.

America's majority religions—in numerical terms the Catholics and in cultural hegemonic terms the Protestants—have always been Utah's minorities: outnumbered, out-financed, and unappreciated. Their sense of social dislocation under Mormon establishment was intensified by their own deep hostility to Mormonism as a belief system. As late as 1905, a Presbyterian divine wrote: "While Christianity is from heaven . . . Mormonism is the monstrous offspring of earth and hell. It is a huge monster that would roll back civilization thousands of years."[19] Given this conviction, it was natural that the most consistent public role of Protestant churches in the Great Basin has been that of opposition to the LDS Church, a righteous opposition determined to heal "this open sore of the world."[20]

Opposition was more than philosophical, however. The first Protestants came to Utah Territory either as representatives of the federal government and appointed to dismantle the Mormon Kingdom or as missionaries for the eastern reform establishment and commissioned to convert Mormons away from Mormonism. The antagonism each denomination had for the other based on experiences in the East was aggravated by the fact that the post-bellum anti-polygamy campaign was supported by allegations and evidence provided by Protestants who lived among the Mormons in the West.

Utah's ministers were extremely popular on the eastern lecture circuit for their dramatic accounts of the evils of Mormonism. Indeed, the major source of funding for their fledgling congregations came from their efforts to convince national mission boards and the Protestant faithful that Mormon barbarism was a threat to the nation. Their efforts contributed to a national press that made the Mormons universal objects of ridicule and scorn. Burlesque treatments in plays and romantic novels made the Mormon man a symbol of unrestrained and predatory sexuality; the Mormon woman a dupe and sexual toy in a mountain harem; and Mormon children the abused and deformed offspring of monstrous parents. A history of intolerance exists in Utah and Idaho that the Mormons have not forgotten, and these cultural memories subtly color their relation to America's mainstream even today. Arguably, Mormonism's twentieth-century display of middle-class values—its emphasis on law-abiding love for country, and even its pride in achievement within the larger culture—reflect an on-going rebuttal to its nineteenth-century experience with Protestant America.

The Protestant campaign had real political consequences for the LDS Church. Beginning with the Morrill Act in 1862, which equated plural marriage with bigamy, cultural norms were coupled with federal legislative might to impose criminal penalties on individual Mormons and political sanctions on Utah Territory. Congress eventually enacted three additional anti-polygamy statutes that successively placed Utah's territorial courts under federal jurisdiction; imposed civil penalties such as disenfranchisement; and simplified proof for polygamy convictions, sending more than 1,000 Latter-day Saints to prison. The courts finally dissolved the corporate status of the LDS Church and confiscated its property. In Idaho, state lawmakers joined federal ones to impose additional burdens on the Latter-day Saints. In 1884, any Idaho citizen affiliated with a group that believed in polygamy was stripped of the right to vote, hold public office, and serve on juries.

Meanwhile, Mormon leadership strategically placed their settlements throughout the territory to check the establishment of non-Mormon ones. Some of the Idaho colonies were meant specifically to "ward off . . . soldier-miners" who expressed an interest in remaining after the Utah War and military occupation of the Utah Territory.[21] Experience had taught the Mormons that it took more than fences to make good neighbors, and so they intended to own all the houses on the block and all the blocks in town. One Mormon leader admitted "we are an aggressive people . . . as we approach the gates of our enemies we buy them out, buy out their ranches, their little settlements."[22]

The religious newcomers were no more inclined to peaceful cohabitation than were the Mormons. In 1897, the Presbytery of Utah, with the endorsement of the Baptists and Congregationalists, printed a pamphlet advising the Christian population of "Ten Reasons Why Christians Cannot Fellowship the Mormon Church."

The Protestant churches were less successful in their missionary work than in their political campaign, however. Several reasons account for their failure. In addition to possessing a negative attitude towards potential proselytes, Protestant missionaries lacked both the personnel and financial resources to adequately sustain a presence in any but the most populated parts of the state. The first permanent non-Mormon worship facility was built by the Congregationalists in Salt Lake City in 1865. Its pastor was Rev. Norman McLeod, who had been sent by the American Home Missionary Society to preach Christianity to Utah and chaplain the army assigned to watch over the Mormon Kingdom. Calling their building "Independence Hall," the Congregationalists shared it with other non-Mormon religions, even the Catholics.

Catholics traveled west with less of a political agenda than the Protestants, and hence have less history of antagonism with the Latter-day Saints. Early Spanish explorers (1776) first claimed the area, but did not settle in Utah's southern deserts, returning to New Mexico instead. The Catholics who came in the next century came to stay, building their first church in 1871. Its pastor arrived two years later to minister to the Catholics among the federal troops stationed in the mountains above Salt Lake City. More Catholics came as the railroad and the mining industries took hold. Since these economic developments were experienced as a threat by the Mormons, the two populations did not mix, often settling as we have seen in different parts of the state. Catholic religious orders followed the faithful to provide pastoral, educational, and medical assistance. In 1908, the Cathedral of St. Mary Magdalene was completed. After its renovation in the 1970s, it continues as a landmark of the Catholic presence in Utah.

Not until the completion of the transcontinental railroad did Protestants come in numbers sufficient to create independent congregations. The first Presbyterian minister arrived a month after the tracks were joined, and by 1870 had organized a congregation at a railroad freight center north of Salt Lake. Likewise, the Episcopalians held their first service in 1867 and opened the first non-Mormon day school by summer. St. Mark's School thrives today as a reminder that, as Bishop Tuttle said, "in Utah, especially, schools were the backbone of our missionary work."[23] A Methodist minister arrived by rail in 1870 and conducted his first service at the Union Pacific and Southern Pacific terminal in Ogden. But the

Protestants arrived too late with too little. In 1896, another Methodist minister reported to his board that although $25 million had been spent on the endeavor, "if two hundred real Mormons have been changed and made into earnest evangelical Christians during [our time here], we have not been able to discover them."[24] When the nineteenth-century gambit of the Protestant establishment to eradicate Mormonism by sword and statute failed, their churches were left as isolated outposts in Mormon country. What has been said of one could be said of all: "Clearly, the Presbyterian cause in Utah was in a state of crisis as the nineteenth century ended."[25]

In part, the Protestants were defeated by their success against polygamy, the end of which also ended donations from the East. In addition, the lack of results from their labors, coupled with the appeal of foreign mission fields, caused the national mission boards to withdraw support. The local representatives of the churches responded to this crisis by combining efforts to minister to their small and scattered flocks. The state was divided and each denomination given responsibility for specific towns. As late as 1930, however, a report on the status of the "Allotment and Occupation of Utah" admitted that entire counties were neglected, such as Morgan County, which had "no Protestant mission. [But] our colporteurs have visited this Country."[26] The sense of "Country," both in terms of size and jurisdictional distinctiveness, helped to defeat all but the most organized Protestant efforts at colonization.

Ultimately, the sub-region's religious warfare was solved by a national political compromise that left the Latter-day Saints' political and economic influence largely intact. In 1907, the U.S. agreed to seat Mormon apostle Reed Smoot in the Senate, and the church subordinated itself to the federal marriage laws. In the exchange, modern Mormonism was born. But the experience of conflict left its mark on all the Great Basin's residents.

Not until 1982 did Idaho repeal its "Test Oath" designed to stop Mormons from voting—and, even then, over opposition from some 100,000 voters and 20 years after similar legislation against Chinese and Native Americans had been repealed. Contemporary research has shown that many Idahoans think the Mormons are coercive and manipulative; that they use political influence to impose Mormon norms on others; and that they use social relationships for the sole purpose of conversion. In addition, a significant portion of the population feel that Mormons judge others and exclude them as inferior.[27]

Attitudes in Utah also reflect continuing religious antagonism. The *Salt Lake Tribune* published results of an elaborate investigation of Utah's interfaith relations on December 9, 2001. Under the title "The Unspoken Divide," the report concluded that Mormons and non-Mormons were separated by a "fault line" recognized by two-thirds of those polled, which "haunt[s] every Utah community" and both sides of the divide. The sentiments of non-Mormons paralleled the Idaho study. Polarized by their demographic and cultural minority status, Utah's non-Mormon population often defines itself in public opposition to the Mormon majority, as seen in litigation over Main Street Plaza in Salt Lake City. Latter-day Saint feelings were not articulated in as much detail as their counterparts. Reference was made, however, to their predictable resentment at being judged negatively for their church-going, child-bearing, alcohol-aversive lifestyle.

Efforts to overcome this polarity constitute one of the central themes of public discourse in the Mormon Corridor. On both sides, religious leaders self-consciously pursue ecumenical efforts. LDS leadership goes to great lengths to share the church's wealth across denominational lines, as shown by contributions to Westminster College (once Presbyterian, but now supported by a consortium of Protestants) and the restoration of Salt Lake City's Catholic Church of the Madeline. Catholics rewarded the LDS Church with an invitation to a member of its First Presidency to participate in its rededication.

But, however ecumenical in spirit, the disparity in size and related sense of powerlessness endures among the Mormon Corridor's other religions. Though, for example, Catholic adherents doubled in the last 10 years, largely through Hispanic immigration, they still constitute a mere 6 percent of total adherents in Utah. During that same period, LDS growth, though at half the rate, raised representation among its adherents from 69 to 87 percent. "We like to say we're the second-largest religious denomination in Utah," Catholic Father Bussen said on February 2, 2002. But, he added, "It's like comparing the size of the mouse to the elephant when they're the only two creatures on earth." The demographic gap and the social-cultural hegemony it supports continues to burden public religion in this sub-region of the Mountain West.

Conclusion

Two basic facts explain the Church of Jesus Christ of Latter-day Saints' enduring power in the Mountain West: one historical, the other theological.

Historically, in America, there were simply too many denominations and too much competition between them for any one to dominate the others. The Latter-day Saints, however, were driven past the edges of America's prairie and found a place that nobody else wanted. To use the old cliché, they turned a lemon into lemonade. Situated between gold mines on the west and rich plains to the east, the Great Basin sheltered Mormonism's establishment in the intermountain West for two generations. Religious pluralism arrived too late and too anemically to vie for the cultural spoils of settlement. Competition for control came most notably from the mining industry, especially in Idaho, and from the U.S. government in Utah. But even America's economic and political power proved insufficient to fully dislodge the Mormons from their Mountain kingdom, though they were required to reform it in the image of American disestablishment.

Notwithstanding its political reformation, the Church of Jesus Christ of Latter-day Saints' contemporary legal battles show that it remains on the edge of what is a permissible relation between American church and state. This cannot be understood without understanding certain fundamental principles of Mormon theology. The LDS Church will remain on the edge of American religious polity as long as it defines its president as a law-giving prophet and its mission as providing temporal order in service to the eternal. Ultimately, the church's claim to sacramental power fuels its economic and political activity and defines its continuing contest with the limits American law sets for American religion. This means, also, that public life in Idaho and Utah will continue to display a quite un-American degree of religious tension and intolerance.

Endnotes

1. I am indebted to Kaye Nickell of Vanderbilt University for her research assistance.
2. D. W. Meinig, "The Mormon Culture Region," *Annals, Association of American Geographers* 55, 2 (1955): 191-220. I am using "core" in the vernacular sense. Technically, for Meinig who discussed the region in terms of "core," "domain," and "sphere" to distinguish population densities in the Mormon Corridor, Utah and southeast Idaho were the "domain" and the Wasatch Front was the core. Today, the Church of Jesus Christ of Latter-day Saints objects to the use of "Mormon Church" as a denominator. It prefers that the institution's entire name be used in order to avoid any inference that the church is not Christian. For the church's guidelines on use of its name, see "Style Guide - The Name of the Church" at http://www.lds.org/(July 5, 2002).
3. In the nineteenth century, the Latter-day Saints often referred to this sub-region as the "Great Basin Kingdom," a name reflecting the domination by the Church of Jesus Christ of Latter-day Saints of political, social, and economic, as well as religious features of the culture. See Leonard J. Arrington, *Great Basin Kingdom: An Economic History of the Latter-day Saints, 1830-1900* (Cambridge, Mass.: Harvard Univ. Press, 1958).
4. Thomas Alexander, *Utah, The Right Place: The Official Centennial History* (Layton, Utah: Gibbs Smith Publisher, 1995), 186. Note, however, other studies indicate that, by the 1970s, concentrations of Mormons within their corridor had increased by 10 percent. "This means," the authors concluded, "that Saints are moving into the core-domain (and probably multiplying) faster than" other identifiable groups. Dean R. Louder and Lowell Bennion,

"Mapping Mormons Across the Modern West," in Richard H. Jackson, ed., *The Mormon Role in the Settlement of the West* (Provo: Brigham Young University Press, 1978), 116-166.

5. Obviously, both the states of Idaho and Utah were originally home to large tribes of Native Americans. Even today, several reservations dot the landscape and native peoples participate in the life of the now European-dominated cultures. The 2000 NARA numbers and the data derived from the 2001 American Religious Identity Survey (ARIS) that provide the basis for this analysis do not provide separate data for Native Americans. Therefore, no account can be given of their religious influence on public life in this sub-region. For a description of the cultural sub-regions within southern Idaho, see Peter Boag's "Mountain, Plain, Desert, River: The Snake River Region as a Western Crossroads," in *Many Wests: Place, Culture, & Regional Identity* (University Press of Kansas, 1997), 180-182.

6. For the purposes of this analysis I have designated the following 15 counties as "southeastern:" Bannock, Bear Lake, Bingham, Bonneville, Butte, Caribou, Cassia, Franklin, Fremont, Jefferson, Madison, Minidoka, Oneida, Power, and Teton. This leaves the following 19 counties in the southwest: Ada, Adams, Blaine, Boise, Camas, Canyon, Clark, Custer, Elmore, Gem, Gooding, Jerome, Lemhi, Lincoln, Owyhee, Payette, Twin Falls, Valley, and Washington. The northern panhandle is comprised of Benewah, Bonner, Boundary, Clearwater, Idaho, Kootenai, Latah, Lewis, Nes Perce, and Shoshone counties.

7. Among the church adherents in Daggett, Piute, and Rich counties, 100 percent are LDS; for Garfield County the ratio dips to 99.5 percent.

8. *Report on the Internal Commerce of the United States for the Year 1890*, as quoted in Lowell C. Bennion, "Mormon Country a Century Ago: A Geographer's View," in Thomas Alexander, ed., *The Mormon People: Their Character and Traditions* (Provo: Brigham Young University Press, 1980), 17.

9. The third most populous county, Kootenai, is in the Idaho panhandle, just east of Spokane, Washington. In the total population, 66.8 percent are unaffiliated or uncounted. Only 13.3 percent are Mormon.

10. I am grateful to Lawrence Coates, Gary Walker, and James Weatherby for help with the Idaho dimension of the story of Mormonism in Idaho's public life.

11. Orson Pratt, quoted in B.H.Roberts, *Comprehensive History of the Church*, 7:515.

12. The bibliography on nineteenth century Mormonism is enormous. A good starting point for a general historical background is Leonard Arrington and Davis Bitton, *The Mormon Experience: A History of the Latter-day Saints* 2nd ed. (Urbana: University of Illinois Press, 1992). For an exhaustive and well organized bibliography of publications on Mormon history and sociology, see

James B. Allen, Ronald W. Walker, and David J. Whittaker, *Studies in Mormon History, 1830-1997: An Indexed Bibliography with a Topical Guide to Published Social Science Literature on the Mormons* (Urbana: University of Illinois Press and BYU Press, 2000).

13. The most recent discussion of the polygamy conflict is Sarah Barringer Gordon *The Mormon Question: Polygamy and Constitutional Conflict in Nineteenth Century America* (Chapel Hill: University of North Carolina Press, 2002).

14. Gordon B. Hinckley interview with Larry King, September 8, 1998. A transcript of the interview is available at http:\\www.lds.org/en/4_News_Update/19980908_CNN_Transcript.html (09/29/98) or see CNN Transcript 98090800V22.

15. Thomas F. O'Dea, *The Mormons* (Chicago: University of Chicago Press, 1957), 173.

16. Jane J. Mansbridge, *Why We Lost the ERA* (Chicago: University of Chicago Press, 1986), 13, 34. Recent books on LDS dissent include John Sillito and Susan Staker, eds., *Mormon Mavericks: Essays on Dissenters* (Salt Lake City: Signature Books, 2002) and James W. Ure, *Leaving the Fold: Candid Conversations with Inactive Mormons* (Salt Lake City: Signature Books, 1999).

17. Arrington, *Great Basin Kingdom*, 34.

18. Robert Gottlieb and Peter Wiley, *America's Saints: the Rise of Mormon Power* (New York: G.P. Putnum & Sons, 1984), 96.

19. Thomas Cary Johnson, *Mormonism* (Richmond: Whittet & Shepperson, Printers, n.d.), 29.

20. E. O. Guerrant, *The Mormons* (Richmond: Whittet & Shepperson, 1899), 12.

21. Bennion, "Mormon Country a Century Ago," 17.

22. Ibid.

23. Quoted in Miriam B. Murphey, "Arrival of the Episcopal Church in Utah, 1867," reprinted in *History Blazer*, October 1995.

24. F. S. Beggs, "The Mormon Problem in the West," *Methodist Review* 78 (September 1896): 755-756.

25. Mark T. Banker, *Presbyterian Missions and Cultural Interaction in the Far Southwest, 1850-1950* (Urbana: University of Illinois Press, 1993), 153.

26. W. M. P[aden], "Notes for a Map of Allotment and Occupation in Utah." Wiley M. Paden Collection, Special Collections, Giovale Library, Westminster College, Salt Lake City, Utah.

27. Keith G. Allred, "Relations Between LDS & Non-LDS Idaho Residents," n.d., copy in author's possession. Used with permission.

Chapter Five

Polarized Tribes: Colorado, Wyoming, and Montana

Philip Deloria

D ifferent sorts of settlements in different places attract different kinds of people. Presumably this leads to different kinds of religious traditions and practices and different sorts of public expression of religion. While some places are easily characterized by religion, the states that join together the northern Rocky Mountains with the edge of the northern Great Plains—Colorado, Wyoming, and Montana—generally appear in surveys and polls as places *without* much religious clarity. That appearance is confirmed experientially.

The South can be seen and experienced in terms of evangelical practice and African-American Protestantism, while the Atlantic states have high proportions of Jewish and Catholic adherents, the product of urban immigration patterns. The Pacific Northwest was settled early and often by Protestant immigrants. And the list can go on: Southern California and Hispanic Catholicism, Southeast Michigan and Islam. Even within the Mountain West region, it is possible to parse out New Mexico and Arizona for the cultural and political weight attached to Hispanic Catholicism and to Native American religions. Utah and Idaho stand out as states in which gravity pulls toward Salt Lake City and the Church of Jesus Christ of Latter-day Saints. In all these places, a general description of region—or sub-region as the case may be—can reasonably be offered by turning, in some part of the definition, to religion.

Colorado, Wyoming, and Montana simply do not fit such a pattern. In some areas within these states, of course, individual religions may dominate. In Butte, Montana, for instance, high proportions of Irish immigrant miners kept Catholicism dominant for much of the late nineteenth and early twentieth century. Now, however, Billings has Montana's largest population of Catholics. Or, one might look across this sub-region and find that a single religious tradition tends to capture a particular social group. Latino residents of these states, as elsewhere, tend to be Catholic (although there is a visible charismatic element among recent Mexican immigrants). In Colorado and Wyoming, the early Episcopalian church did a good job capturing economic elites, who have always been and continue to be a mainstay of that church. Patterns such as these can be found across all three states.

The general rule for Colorado, Wyoming, and Montana, however, is scattered enclaves, diversity, pluralism, overlaps, transformations in and contests among various religious practices. Though the dominant religious tradition in most of Montana's 57 counties is Catholic, for example (with a substantial portion of Lutherans), the state is also home to Hutterites, Mennonites, and Amish, each deeply impelled to enclave, separate, and govern themselves on restrictive religious grounds.[1] Throughout the sub-region, Mormon influence on the counties bordering Utah and Idaho has waxed and waned and waxed again over time.

Region itself can be a vexed concept. How can enough commonality across a geographic space be established in order to fit Colorado, Wyoming, and Montana together into a category here called a "sub-region"? Moreover, how can that coherence be related to the question of religion?

One place to start is shared physical characteristics, especially the Rocky Mountains and the Continental Divide, which run through all three states. As is true elsewhere in this region, the mountains, gorges, rapidly running streams, and the meadows scattered among the mountains have a quasi-sacred power that has affected the religious ambiance of this particular sub-region. Each of these three states has substantial plains, prairie, and basin regions. Each has experience with extractive economies—gold, silver, and molybdenum in Colorado; gold and copper in Montana; coal, oil, and gas in Wyoming. Each has been a transportation corridor or crossroads.

After a long career hosting the fur trade, overland migration, and the rush to Montana's goldfields, for example, Wyoming was seriously settled in order to support the initial transcontinental railroad. Its two most important urban centers—Cheyenne and Laramie—began as "end camps" on the Union Pacific. Montana got the last transcontinental, but it also had the distinction of having not one but two of them—the Great Northern and the Northern Pacific—and its settlement patterns speak volumes about these railroads' recruitment of ethnic Europeans and their religious traditions to the northern Great Plains. In Colorado, the corridor that includes Boulder and Colorado Springs sits astride the great North-South-East-West crossroads of the plains, formed first as trails up and down the Front Range of the Rockies, then later as railroad lines, and now as Interstate highways 25 and 70.

Each area dealt quickly and often violently with its indigenous populations, although each state continues to be characterized by important enclaves of Indian people whose religion, traditionally and in the present, stands at the very core of their being. Each state has substantial acreage controlled by the federal government in the form of the National Park Service, the U.S. Forest Service, the Bureau of Reclamation, and the Bureau of Land Management. They all have significant agricultural, ranching, mining, and tourist industries. Each tends to be one of the so-called "blue states"—those that vote reliably Republican in national elections—a label that often masks political complexity at the state and local level. Each plays host to a number of diverse religious traditions—Catholic, Protestant, Jewish, in all their forms— but also a plethora of other practices and newly forming spiritual traditions, as well as a range of still-vital Native-American religions.

But from the religious perspective it is important to recognize that, like the rest of the states in the Mountain West—all except Utah, which is nearly always a special case—a substantial percentage of the population of this sub-region fits into the "None" category. Almost 55 percent of Colorado's total population is religiously unaffiliated; in Wyoming, the percentage is 50.6; and in Montana, the percentage is 52.9.

Because the religious configuration and religio-spiritual atmosphere in these three states differ too much from state to state and place to place to permit broad generalization, even at the state level, this chapter begins with an examination of religion in Boulder and Colorado Springs, two Colorado cities where differences are so marked that these two places seem to belong to quite separate and distinct universes. Then the chapter moves forward to yet another universe: Native-American religious traditions and the changes those traditions have undergone in the century and a half since European-American culture made its way into the Northern Rockies. After that, the chapter returns to more familiar territory—the appearance and development in this region of churches and denominations that are present throughout every part of the United States—before concluding with a survey of the recent and even current religious scene in Colorado, Wyoming, and Montana.

A Tale of Two Cities

When Thomas Aikens and his Nebraska gold seekers entered the Boulder valley in 1859, they were not likely thinking about establishing a place of diverse and cosmopolitan religious practice. The miners had faith—in the possibility of gold and their own advancement into the ranks of self-made men—but like other miners across the West, their heavenly reward took a back seat to earthly advancement. Aikens' party stood in stark contrast to the local Arapahoe people, who managed for a few more years to maintain their seasonal and sacred rounds through the valley. They were driven out in 1864 by the Methodist parson turned military commander, John Chivington, who led Boulder and Denver men to the notoriously brutal Sand Creek Massacre.

After a quick boom/bust cycle, the miners' discovery of silver (1869) and tellurium (1872) lured farmers and mercantilists to the valley. They supplied the mines while also establishing the first Catholic (1877) and mainline Protestant churches in the area. Subsequent immigrants to the mines and fields brought a range of denominational diversity to Boulder. In addition to Congregationalists (1868), Methodists (1872), Presbyterians (1876), and Episcopalians (1875, 1879), in Boulder there were Swedish Lutherans (1896), Seventh-day Baptists (1893), Christian Scientists (1926), and still later, the Church of Christ, Pilgrim Holiness, Foursquare Gospel, Jehovah's Witnesses, Church of the Nazarene, and others. Seventh-day Adventists founded a sanitarium in Boulder, which prefigured the town's later image in its emphasis on health food and whole grain cereals.

Populations of African Americans (about 300 people, or 1 percent of Boulder's population, according to the 1880 census), Chinese immigrants, and Latinos settled along Boulder Creek, bringing to the town sparsely documented practices of Hispanic Catholicism and various Eastern religions. The African Methodist congregation, after years of meeting in rented space, built its own church in 1884. Farther out in the county, Japanese farmers created the area's first Buddhist shrines. By the early twentieth century, Boulder's geography was marked by numerous official churches—many the imposing stone replacements for first drafts in wood—and no doubt many unofficial ones. Boulder's early story—of mining boom and bust, agricultural diversification, local political hegemony, and diverse immigration and settlement—was not radically dissimilar from any number of Mountain West towns. Indeed, one finds similar or parallel trajectories in Butte, Billings, Helena, and Bozeman in Montana; and in Laramie and Cheyenne in Wymoing, among others.

Between 1907 and 1913, Boulder's city leaders, intuiting the end of the mining boom that built the city, and seeing a limited future in agricultural supply, self-consciously sought to remake Boulder as a "city beautiful," the imagined "Athens of the West." They shifted the town's orientation away from the mines and mills and toward the Flatirons, impressive rock formations at the base of the nearby mountains, and they began—publicly and collectively—to imagine a romantic, sublime landscape, one that would be seen for the next century, often by the unchurched, as sacred and spiritual. By the 1970s, this sublime landscape would inspire a wash of spiritual seekers from the counterculture and the budding New Age movement. Buddhists arrived in force in the early 1970s, as Chogyam Trunpa Rinpoche established a monastery in the nearby hills and, in 1974, the Naropa Institute (later University), which fused religious instruction with a cultural avant-garde that included poets, psychologists, composers, filmmakers, and writers.

Underestimating the power of Naropa in setting a cultural tone for the town would be difficult: visitors like Allen Ginsberg and William Burroughs mingled with serene Buddhists and New Agers, spawning a culture that smiled on health food stores, personal improvement classes, and an easy-access religious potpouri. The sacralized landscape drew the followers of the Maharishi Mahesh Yogi (known for Transcendental Meditation), and those of the Bhagwan Shree Rajneesh, who dressed only in the oranges and yellows of sunset, and were easily confused, in some minds, with a small but visible Sikh community.

The mountain climbers who frequented Boulder established a pipeline to friends in Tibet and Nepal. Tibetan immigrants established their own community, a "Little Tibet" with its own religious practice. Indeed, out of the 38 major Buddhist centers listed in Colorado today, more than a quarter are located in Boulder (including several devoted to various lineages of Tibetan Buddhism).[2] New Age spiritual practices, with their multicultural melange of spiritual traditions, thrived in the area. In 2000, the only place in the northern Rockies with a statistically visible population of Muslims was Boulder County. And there are not many towns in the region where monthly Wicca meetings are advertised with such delight.

In spite of this astonishing religious diversity, mainline churches maintained their historic importance. Boulder was once a quieter place, well suited for the Convent of St. Walburga, a cloister on South Boulder Road maintained by Benedictine nuns from 1935 till 1997.[3] The Mount St. Gertrude Catholic Girls School that had once anchored the University Hill neighborhood and Sacred Heart Catholic continued the tradition on the north side of town. Downtown, First Presbyterian Church pulled in thousands of members, expanding several times until it overflowed its block and built annexes nearby. St. John's Episcopal remained a church of choice for many local elites. In 1997, it found itself in the center of a national debate for its congregation's support of John and Patsy Ramsey, suspected in the death of their daughter, Jon Benet. Lutherans, Methodists, and Catholics all maintained multiple churches with large congregations.

Of churches and denominations whose institutional judicatories reported membership statistics that became the basis of the North American Religion Atlas (NARA) in 2000, 36.2 percent of all adherents in Boulder County were Catholic. Almost 46 percent of Protestant adherents were connected to institutions in historic mainline denominations or other mainline Protestant or liberal Christian denominations. But slightly more that 54 percent of all Protestant adherents were connected to institutions that either were part of such traditionally conservative denominations as the Moravians and Nazarenes, or else with the new evangelical groups. Among the latter were the Creekside Evangelical Church (associated with the "Shepherd's Fellowship"), the Calvary Bible Church, and a Vineyard Church in North Boulder with a fellowship on the campus of the University of Colorado.

The university campus is also the site where Navigators, Intervarsity, Campus Crusade, and other organizations seek out student followers. In March 1990, with the help of a Campus Crusade leader and two other close friends, the university's football coach, Bill McCartney, gathered a group of 72 men at the Boulder Valley Christian Church to discuss a conference for the men of Colorado. The six dozen men committed to pray and fast on Wednesdays for this conference, which would be held in July 1991. The name Promise Keepers evolved out of messages centered on personal integrity that "Coach Mac" had given at a number of churches along the Front Range of Colorado. A board of directors was developed, and Promise Keepers was incorporated in the state of Colorado in December of 1990. Although it seems to have lost some of its steam, for a time this organization was virtually the quintessential evangelical organization for men, not just in the Mountain West, but throughout the nation. When it established headquarters, however, Denver rather than Boulder became its home base.

Upon its already-diverse roots, Boulder, by the 1980s and 1990s, had built a new tradition of religious diversity characterized by openness and syncretism, actualized by a complex mixture of loose collectives, structured institutions, and organized religious communities. It had become a place of religious pluralism, built around familiar congregations, to be sure, but also out of charismatic leaders, exotic practices, individual self-actualization, and a landscape thought to evoke— or be—sacred. Religious refugees sought it out for its beauty, its reputation for tolerance, and its religious cosmopolitanism.

Colorado Springs had similar beginnings—a brief fling with mining around 1860 and then a turn to agriculture, ranching, and, most particularly, tourism. In 1871, William Jackson Palmer founded Colorado Springs as a health resort community. He built good railroad connections and insisted upon wide streets, plentiful trees and parks, spacious views, clean industry, temperance, and churches of many denominations. British financial backing and a strenuous recruiting effort brought so many English immigrants that, for a time, "Little London" was the nickname of the town that stood at the base of Pike's Peak. Except for the English Gothic Grace Episcopal Church that was built on Pike's Peak Avenue in 1873, however, not much evidence suggests that the Britishers' Anglicanism had much long-lasting effect on religion in Colorado Springs.[4]

The nearby Manitou Hot Springs helped make the area a popular location for sanitariums, and the Broadmoor Hotel became a nationally famous luxury vacation retreat in the 1920s. Indeed, an early tourist economy succeeded in Colorado Springs in ways that it never did in Boulder. A significant part of the labor for that economy was African American—by 1900 over 1,000 African-American people lived in El Paso County, with accompanying African Methodist and African Methodist Episcopal churches.

But in the late nineteenth century, Boulder was awarded the state university—which contributed to its "city beautiful" emphasis—while Colorado Springs' near-neighbor, Canon City, received the state prison—a harbinger of a public sector economy to come. While tourism remained—and remains—an important part of the Colorado Springs economy, by the mid-twentieth century the city began turning increasingly, not simply to the state, but to the federal pot. The city bought and donated land and successfully lobbied for Fort Carson, an Army training base founded in 1942. It was also home to Peterson Air Force Base (1942), and, its real coup, North American Air Defense Command (NORAD) headquarters (1958), with its operations center built underneath nearby Cheyenne Mountain, and the United States Air Force Academy, which also opened in 1958.

In the 1980s, Schriever Air Force Base joined these others. Like many western towns at mid-century, Colorado Springs tied itself to federal military expenditures—but it did so with a stunning effectiveness that exceeded its rivals. By the 1980s, these five major facilities made 60 percent of the Springs' economy military-related. As important, the sheer demographic weight of the military presence began tilting the culture of the town away from a tourist service economy—which inevitably tends toward the tolerant—and toward a certain Cold War conservatism. Many military retirees found the town a congenial home, and their presence helped consolidate a cultural climate very different from that being developed in Boulder. Catholic and mainline Protestant churches, not surprisingly, were the general rule.

Faced in the early 1980s with a troubled economy, a collapsed real estate market, and the threat of military budget cuts, Colorado Springs' leaders cast about for new forms of economic development and decided to recruit evangelical Christian organizations. Christian groups, they decided, would pump the economy, function in post-industrial ways that did not adversely affect the beauty of the surroundings, and dovetail nicely with the conservative character of the town. In short order, Colorado Springs became home to a number of groups with the resources and the will to intervene in national, state, and local political culture. Perhaps the largest and most significant of these organizations was Focus on the Family, a California group organized in 1977.

Led by Dr. James Dobson, it was recruited with the aid of a $4-million grant from a local foundation. Built in 1995, the organization's headquarters on the north side of town, employs some 900 people producing radio shows, leaflets, books, television, and Internet and other media focusing on the celebration, maintenance, and defense of what it views as the "traditional" family.[5]

The Navigators and Younglife, two successful evangelical Christian youth organizations, the International Bible Society, the Family Research Institute, and many others joined Dobson's group, making Colorado Springs one of the centers of the so-called Christian right. By the mid-1990s, nearly 100 such organizations of varying sizes were operating out of Colorado Springs.

Quickly, the "Springs" became Boulder's opposite, at least in terms of the public and political expression of religious belief. Where the latter embodied a left-liberal politics, the former became the power base for conservative Republican politics in Colorado. From the city at the base of Pike's Peak came a torrent of words, candidates, and referendums dealing with everything from traditional hot-button issues such as abortion, homosexuality, and school prayer to term limit plans and radical tax reform measures.

To residents of Boulder, the politics of El Paso County often seemed driven by a monolithic, conspiratorial, and crude Christian fundamentalism. Yet, in the Springs itself, one found—and still finds—a complex brew of fundamentalist and mainline religious traditions, with alliances forming, fragmenting, and reforming all the time. The city's politics actually intermingled several different *kinds* of conservativism—economic, social, individualist, and religious—that are characteristic of other parts of the Mountain West region.

Indeed, some have suggested that the *schisms* in this political formation have prevented substantive change on the model of Christian fundamentalism. That judgment depends on where one is standing. It is certainly the case that the political culture of Colorado has in fact been visibly transformed by the specific concentration of religious right organizations recruited to El Paso County. And it is likely that the political culture has, in some measure, influenced other religious-political groups within the region, and indeed, the nation as a whole.

According to his followers, over 7.5 million people hear James Dobson's daily radio show each week. Since the Focus message goes out over 3,000 radio stations in North America, and 3,300 worldwide, in 15 different languages, it seems likely that the political reach of this group extends far beyond the bounds of Colorado, and even beyond the Mountain West region. Tom Minnery, a Focus official, outlined the organization's political and cultural agenda in bald terms, observing that "government is an institution that has been established by God, and we ought to care as much about that institution as we do about the institution of the church."[6]

How might this tale of two cities help us think about religion within the northern Mountain West sub-region? Each place encapsulates a number of important impulses in American religious practice, impulses that may help us make sense out of the northern Rockies, an area that lacks much of the organizing clarity found in other places. Both Boulder and Colorado Springs function as enclaves, protected spaces with sometimes visible and coherent religious boundaries that contribute to collective senses of local identity. At the same time, however, both cities transcend their own boundaries, with Boulder drawing in unto itself a wide array of global religious practice, and Colorado Springs aggressively reaching out to the world through political, cultural, and religious proselytizing. Colorado Springs often seems dogmatic and intolerant, willing to prescribe its own beliefs and practices as *the* single social standard. Boulder appears just the opposite—relativist, open to any and all kinds of diverse practice, and reluctant to impose social standards.

Yet the seeming unanimity of Colorado Springs' political voices masks a mild diversity of belief and practice among evangelical organizations, often made visible in political differences. And the apparent libertarianism and tolerance of pluralist Boulder masks any number of rigid orthodoxies in that city. Boulder residents can be dogmatic, prescriptive, and intolerant—in insisting on their particular brand of tolerance. The West in general, and in recent years the northern Rockies in particular, is often imagined as Boulder: an escape, a refuge, a possibility, a place where one might carve out a space for one's own quasi-secular, multicultural spiritual practices. On the other hand, the West and the northern Rockies have also truly been like Colorado Springs—a place of enclaves, of prescriptive mandates, of dogma, rigidity, and sometimes, intolerance.

Yet, as is suggested here, if these two cities are used to make visible certain tropes—the creation of enclaves, prescription and proscription, global reach, multi-tradition mingling of religious practice—their contrasts and contradictions can serve as a reminder that those tropes are always more complicated on the ground, as it were. Perhaps as much as anywhere else in the United States, the northern Mountain West region is a place for seeing the complex working out of religious practices negotiated between libertarian tolerance and prescriptive desires for a single way of believing. The region's enclaves—be they Indian reservation, wealthy New Age retreat, Hispanic Catholic town, Hutterite compound, evangelical business community—are simultaneously connected, and distanced from the surrounding world. They often embrace dogmatic positions, while at the same time debating those very same positions. And this simultaneity of isolation and connection has emerged out of the diverse history of settlement that characterizes Colorado, Wyoming, and Montana.

Native American Religious Tradition and Change

Within Colorado, there are two Indian reservations, for the Ute Mountain and Southern Ute tribes, located in the southwest corner of the state. In Wyoming, the Wind River reservation, near—and larger than—Yellowstone National Park, is home to Shoshone and Arapaho people. Montana has seven relatively large reservations. The Blackfeet reservation borders Glacier National Park and is about the same size. East of Blackfeet lies Rocky Boy, Fort Belknap (home to Gros Ventres and Assiniboine), and Fort Peck (home to northern Sioux). Further south are reservations belonging to the Flathead, Crow, and Northern Cheyenne.

Each of these places has a diverse history, as do the Indian people who occupy them. Almost all of these peoples had—and continue to have—spiritual and subsistence relationships with the plains and with mountains of their homelands. Specific places matter. They are sacred and are, if not exactly parallel, certainly analogous to churches in the Christian sense.

In many of the Plains Indian traditions that continue to characterize most of the Montana and Wyoming reservations, spiritual insight comes to a person after a vision quest, a ritual of sacrifice and self-deprivation that leads to the granting of power to an individual. A vision requires the interpretation of community elders, and often a performance by the community itself in order to insure that power granted to a specific person is used to benefit the whole. Likewise, certain community rituals—most notably the Sun Dance among northern Plains peoples— take power from the great mystery and diffuse it across the earth and among the people through the sacrifice of individual dancers. If places matter to Indian people, then, so too do specific rituals, objects, and songs.

In hastening the late nineteenth century settlement of the Mountain West states, federal and state governments first sought the military defeat or intimidation of these tribes, then their confinement within bounded reservations, and finally the transformation of their cultural beliefs, most particularly their religious traditions. Mainline Christian missionaries were to convert and "civilize" Indian people in one convenient action. Episcopalians, Catholics, Presbyterians, Congregationalists, and Methodists, among others, all established missions in the states of the northern mountains and plains, and they sought to replace rituals and beliefs with Christian practice. Religious boarding schools and day schools tried to change Indian dress and habits while teaching a curriculum that mingled Christianity with agricultural and industrial skills best suited to menial labor. With the aid of the federal government, missionaries denied Indians the free exercise of religion, passing laws and regulations prohibiting dancing and other ceremonies.

Not surprisingly, given this history, some Native people view Christianity as a hostile, colonial, religious tradition. In many places, however, Indian Christianity became a sincere and important substitute for older Indian political orders, which had also been disrupted by reservations. Indian Christian leaders, such as the Arapaho priest Sherman Coolidge, became voices for native people in both the region and the nation. Locally, religious convocation gatherings stood in for the Sun Dance or other ceremonies in some places; men's and women's societies reproduced older warrior and social societies. Church services might even stand in for social dances and meetings, and many native societies across the West developed real affection for Christian hymn singing.[7] For much of the twentieth century, one could argue, Indian Christianity—wherever it could be locally controlled by Indian worshipers, priests, and lay officials—actually worked to preserve older Indian cultural practices.

The spiritual havoc wreaked through the partnership between missionaries and federal government must not be underestimated. Efforts at conversion often worked to turn reservations into religious ghettos. At the same time, however, Indian peoples' ability to make their worlds over must also not be underestimated. Both historically and at the present time, Indian people have tended to function in terms of *parallelism of belief and practice*—that is, it is quite possible for the same person to attend a Christian church on Sunday, a Native American Church meeting on Monday, a traditional spiritual gathering on Tuesday, and so on. At the same time, the colonial context surrounding religious practice has also given rise to *hybrid* or *synthetic* forms of religious practice. (Of these, the Native American Church, which mingles together Christian understandings with the use of peyote as a sacred sacrament, is perhaps the most prominent, with chapters on most western reservations.) Throughout the twentieth century, Indian Christians—and indeed Indian clergy—often served as the most important interface between state and local governments and Indian people.

These kinds of connections between politics, Christian religion, and social relations came into question at mid-century. The 1934 Indian Reorganization Act placed political power in the hands of tribal councils rather than Indian religious figures, and new political leaders banded together in pan-Indian organizations such as the National Congress of American Indians (1944), needed to fight off attempts to "terminate" tribal status in the 1950s. At midcentury, Indian people created a "culture of politics" that displaced religious concerns in favor of pragmatic work within the apparatus of the New Deal state. The civil rights activism of the 1960s, made most visible in the activities of the American Indian Movement (AIM), sought to put into place a "politics of culture," in which religious belief and practice figured in critical ways.

By the 1970s, "termination" had been replaced by a new policy of Self Determination, which has since become an important occasion for Indian people to assert control over their own lives and resources. Key to the Indian political and economic transformations during the last 30 years has been the restoration of older religious practices. Native believers reclaimed all manner of traditional practices. In many cases, these persistent and newly (re)empowered religious ceremonies sit at the core of contemporary controversies involving native people in the states of the Rockies and the Plains.

Unlike Christianity, many Native religious practices are not geographically transportable, but based in and on particular and specific places. For Montana's Northern Cheyenne, for example, South Dakota's Bear Butte is of critical importance in their cosmology.[8] Every native group has a number of sacred sites, and gaining access to them at certain times of the year has proved critical and difficult. Wyoming's Devil's Tower, for instance, has been the site of numerous struggles, court cases, and policy directives regarding access. Known as Mato Tipila Paha (Hill of the Bear's Lodge) by the Lakota, the volcanic outcropping is critical to ceremonies during the month of June, when Lakota believers find it a nodal point in the annual transfer of power from the Great Mystery to the earth.

As rock climbing has become increasingly popular, Devil's Tower has become a favorite destination, and climbers were for many years notably insensitive to the religious practices of Indian people. From their vantage points, climbers observe ceremonies. They would yell and holler to one another, and sometimes to people on the ground. The National Park Service proposed a climbing ban during the month of June, and while many climbers found this a not unreasonable compromise, others protested vehemently, sometimes claiming—in a distinctly "Boulder" manner—that their own act of recreational climbing had religious significance. The climbing ban is currrently voluntary, and while the number of June climbers has decreased climbing—and its resultant disruption—has not stopped. Most struggles are less dramatic, but they play out in many places throughout the Mountain West, particularly where public land status gives open access to sites that Indian people would prefer to be restricted, or where private status prevents Indian people from visiting sacred sites necessary to the practice of their religion.[9]

Other conflicts have taken place around the actual practice of Native-American religions. New Age adherents (such as one might easily find in Boulder) have claimed that any attempt to keep them from appropriating Indian religious practice represents an infringement on their First Amendment right to free practice of religion. Though Indian people in the late 1980s and early 1990s issued a number of "Declarations of War" on New Age appropriations, they have been unable to counter this argument in a juridical context.

These struggles have played out in the political arena in curious venues like the National Eagle Repository in Denver. In 1940, the Bald Eagle Protection Act prevented anyone, except Indian people, from possessing any part of an eagle. Native people have long used eagle feathers, wings, bones, and other parts as powerful ceremonial objects, and the repository has functioned as a clearinghouse, matching up dead eagles with requests from tribal permit-holders. The wait for eagle parts has been about three years. In 2002, however, non-Indians who claimed to be following Indian religious practice challenged the system, claiming that their right to worship was being violated. The U.S. Supreme Court refused to take the case, letting a lower court victory stand for the plaintiffs.

Not surprisingly, the Court and Congress have not done particularly well by Indians. In 1978, Congress passed the American Indian Religious Freedom Act

(AIRFA), which meant to protect the practice of Native religious traditions, most particularly from regulatory impingements by federal agencies. The law was passed, however, without enforcement provisions, and it has been gutted by a series of court decisions that have asserted once again the government's right to impose restrictions on Native American religious practice.

In *Lyng v. Northwest Indian Cemetery Protective Association* (1988), the Supreme Court ruled that Indian people had to prove that, in making a complaint under AIRFA, they had either been coerced into violating their beliefs or penalized for practicing them, a different standard than the "free exercise of religion" standard articulated for others. The immediate result was the denial of access rights and carte blanche for government-sanctioned destruction of sacred sites through, in the *Lyng* case, the opening of an area to logging.

In a 1990 case (*Employment Division, Department of Human Resources of Oregon v. Alfred L. Smith*), the Court made it clear that the "war on drugs" could be judged a more compelling interest than the free practice of religion, as expressed through the use of peyote in Native American Church rituals. (AIRFA, however, was amended in 1993 to codify protections for peyote use by members of the Church.)[10]

Some of the most controversial intersections of religious and political debate have occurred around the 1990 Native American Graves Protection and Repatriation Act (NAGPRA). Under NAGPRA, tribes, states, and museums have been forced to work together to protect funerary remains and sacred objects. Frequently, this has meant the removal of remains and objects from museums, either for reburial or for a different kind of custodial relationship. Museums and curators have worried that NAGPRA opens the door to widespread claims on their collections by Native people.

The Denver Art Museum, with its rich collecting history, has been a leader in establishing common ground with tribes, but not all institutions have been so willing to repatriate holdings. The museum hired a Native American repatriation coordinator, Roger Echo-Hawk, who worked hard to integrate the spiritual necessities of NAGPRA claimants with assistance in confronting the technical difficulties of claim submission. NAGPRA put stress on tribes, requiring the creation of cultural affairs officers and engagement with new tangles of bureaucracy. The Denver museum's experience, which has tried to emphasize partnership, assistance, and mutual respect, has suggested that—contrary to the fears of museum professionals—tribes do not aim to clear out museum holdings, but rather are often interested in a limited number of objects only.

While some tribes have shied away from human remains, others have seen repatriation and reburial of ancestral remains a critical act of spiritual obligation. In Washington state, the 1996 discovery of "Kennewick Man," a 9,000-year-old skeleton with supposed "Caucasoid"—note, *not* "Caucasian"—features became a focal point for debates concerning NAGPRA, with tribal people requesting the skeleton for sacred reburial, and scientists insisting on keeping it for further study. A long history of scientific skull hunting and looting of Indian burials did not soften Indian people toward the scientists' position.[11]

Within Colorado, Wyoming, and Montana, reservation geographies reflect unique religious spaces. They function, on the one hand, as enclaves capable of consolidating and affirming Native religious practice. They can be communities of the culturally like-minded, with long traditions of prescriptive social behavior and shaming practices to enforce conformity to a cultural standard uniquely different from the surrounding areas. On the other hand, they can also be seen as cosmopolitan spaces, constantly dealing with influences from the outside, including the missionary efforts of Mormons and Christian evangelicals, the hybrid influence of the Native American Church, the passing through of curious multicultural gleaners of exotic religious practice.

Because Native people have codified treaty agreements with the United States government (and therefore formal political relations), religious issues can often place them in compromised positions, with their desire for religious freedom conflicting with—and usually losing to—other kinds of national legal and political imperatives.

The "War on Drugs," it turns out, can mean more than Indian religious practice. So does the right of a federal agency to encourage logging, or the right of a university to build a telescope on private land. Or the right of scientists to claim a skeleton. Or the right of rock climbers to ascend a piece of stone because climbers believe that rock climbing is a secular form of religious experience. The resulting political and legal conflicts are very much about maintaining "tradition"—in the form of religion and culture—in the midst of powerful forces for change.

The Creation of a Catholic/Protestant Mainline

Mainline congregations did not simply appear along with the first miners and settlers. The early accounts of mineral rushes and settlements suggest very little in the way of organized religion. Rather, churches were established in Colorado, Wyoming, and Montana through three primary vectors, which can be seen in terms of the interlocked geographies of Indian missions, circuit riding, and transportation corridors. President Ulysses Grant's "Peace Policy" of the 1870s gave power to religious denominations to run reservation agencies. Grant hoped that this measure would clear out corrupt and incompetent agents and place committed Christians in charge. Across the West, Methodists were given 14 Indian agencies, Northern Baptists five, Congregationalists three, Episcopalians eight, and so on.

Catholics, who had prior claims on 42 Indian agencies, were awarded only seven, which led them to establish their own contract school system.

As Ferenc Szasz points out, the policy produced competition among denominations, while also building denominational commitment to certain reservations and peoples. Thanks to the labors of the missionary John Roberts, for example, Wyoming's Wind River reservation became a highly Episcopalian space.[12] Montana's Crow reservation witnessed intense competition between Catholic and Baptist missionaries in the late nineteenth century, before transforming into a pluralistic spiritual setting with plenty of emphasis on refigured Crow traditions.[13]

As elsewhere, Indian missionary efforts in the Mountain West often morphed into the founding of churches that really served nearby white settlements. Reservations, however, did not structure the bulk of early church building in Colorado, Wyoming, and Montana.

That distinction goes to circuit riding church founders. While itinerant preachers had made the rounds of the first gold strikes in the early 1860s, it was not until the latter part of the decade that missionary founders began to have a real impact. Seeing the West as a land of spiritual opportunity—and sectarian competition— mobile missionaries quickly sought to establish congregations, sometimes with only minimal numbers of people. Missionaries such as the Presbyterian Sheldon Jackson sought out a few families of their denomination, quickly organized a church, and then hit the road again. According to Szasz, in one busy stretch, Jackson organized seven churches in 16 days. Though many of his churches collapsed as settlers moved on, Jackson-founded churches lasted in Rawlings, Cheyenne, and Laramie, Wyoming; and in Bozeman and Helena, Montana.

Such missionaries worked hand-in-hand with railroads and land developers, who had strong incentives for offering settlers the image of stability and civilization carried by a church. Accordingly, railroad and town corporations often gave lots to almost every church requesting one, producing sometimes unjustified proliferations of churches. Boulder's church boom of the 1870s mirrored that of many towns in the Rockies, for instance. In Boulder County, the struggle for a county government center had been concluded, but land speculation continued—and even intensified. Boulder had won out and, its future relatively certain, had become an attractive place for serious church building.

The same was essentially true in Laramie, Cheyenne, Rock Springs, and Casper in Wyoming; Butte, Helena, Bozeman, Billings, and Great Falls in Montana; and Denver, Colorado Springs, Pueblo, Julesburg, and Grand Junction in Colorado. The organization of congregations and construction of sanctuaries took place anywhere local or regional political power had been concentrated.

In most cases, those places were connected to the outside world by railroad lines and market relationships. Perhaps nowhere was this pattern so pronounced as in Montana, where two different railroad lines established different kinds of settlement. James J. Hill's Great Northern was America's only privately built transcontinental, and he was able to pull off the feat through sophisticated recruitment of European migrants, many of whom saw in Montana a refuge where they could practice ethnicity, culture, and religion unbothered. Germans (including those from Russia), Slavs, and others made up the lightly populated northern tier of the Rockies.

Following the model of the Midwest, which linked church-building to the founding of religious colleges, missionaries inaugurated a number of small private schools in the Mountain West. These institutions were meant, in the best tradition of religious prescription, to mold the unshaped character of the Mountain West. As E.P. Tenney, president of Colorado College (Congregationalist, in Colorado Springs) pointed out in 1877, "It will be impossible to plant a Christian College in Colorado without doing much thereby toward modifying the future of New Mexico, Arizona, Utah, Wyoming, and every nearby state in the region."[14]

Episcopalians founded private academies across the West, including those in Laramie (St. Matthews Hall, 1895), Denver (Wolfe Hall, 1899) and Golden, Colorado (St. Matthews, 1886). Though many of the denominational colleges clustered in Kansas and Nebraska, one could find collegiate programs in Billings (Rocky Mountain College), Laramie (Laramie Baptist Academy), and Denver (Iliff Theological).

Few of these colleges succeeded over the long term, suggesting just how misplaced was the optimism that the Rockies and Plains would be settled to the density of the Midwest or East. Nonetheless, in the movement to build educational institutions, one can see both the fear that the West would become too much like latter-day Boulder, an open territory for the unchurched and the heretical, and the response, which looked a lot like that of latter-day Colorado Springs, with its emphasis on education and social-political transformation.

Transformations

Tracking religious census data collected over the last half of the twentieth century, it is possible to see the ways that the early development of the northern Rockies continues to shape religious practice—and the ways in which recent history has opened up different paths. In 1952, though all three states had a majority of counties in which Catholicism predominated, as a result of several patterns of historical religious migration. Colorado, Wyoming, and Montana looked very different from one another. The vast majority of Montana was Catholic, the result of the predominantly Catholic immigrants settled by railroads and the Irish, Italian, and eastern European immigrants who populated the mining regions.

Northeastern Montana, on the other hand, looked somewhat different, demonstrating a surge of Lutheran influence moving west from Minnesota and the Dakotas. In addition to five predominantly Lutheran counties in the state's northeast corner, six additional Lutheran counties dotted the state, with single Presbyterian and Methodist counties cropping up in isolated rural areas. In the remaining 44 counties, Catholicism claimed the largest number of adherents.

Twelve of Wyoming's 23 counties were predominantly Catholic, including those containing the prominent towns of Laramie, Cheyenne, Casper, Gillette, Sheridan, and Rock Springs. Four counties adjoining or near Utah and Idaho had a majority of Latter-day Saints, which comes as no surprise, while two other counties showed the results of Congregationalist missionary activities. The counties containing the relatively smaller towns of Douglas and Worland had a majority of Methodists but, as would be expected, Yellowstone National Park remained unchurched.

Although Montana and Wyoming had many Protestant congregations whose members worshipped in Protestant structures, Catholicism carried much of the weight and power in both states. The same is true in Colorado. But Colorado's history also reflects more sustained demographic growth and a larger population, both historically and in the present. Since that growth has been accompanied by a relatively greater variety of religious movements into the area, the state has always been more diverse than the other two states in the sub-region.

Take Colorado's San Luis valley, for example. Founded in 1851, the small town of San Luis is the oldest non-Indian settlement in Colorado. Its initial settlement was driven by late colonial Hispanic Catholic movement north from New Mexico, and the town was laid out on a "Spanish" model, with the gothic adobe Sangre de Cristo parish church (now the mother institution for eight mission churches) completed in 1886. But during the late nineteenth and twentieth centuries, the region also saw the arrival, with various waves of immigrants, of Mormonism, a number of mainline Protestant denominations, and later of charismatic and pentecostal practices, many carried to the valley by new migrants from Mexico.

Towering above the town today is the Shrine of the Stations of the Cross, an enormous series of sculptures built on a flat mesa overlooking San Luis. A mile-long trail leads one through the stations to a final sculpture ("the Resurrection") and a grotto devoted to Our Lady of Guadalupe.[15] Visually, the Shrine defines the town in terms of Hispanic Catholicism, but it does so in a commercial way that reflects a serious infusion of religious modernism into what residents would see as a deeply traditional Catholic practice. Clearly, San Luis functions both as an enclave of Catholicism and as a diverse religious space, open and connected to outside influence.

Summarizing the Colorado situation: as with the San Luis valley (which incorporates a number of Colorado counties) a significant number of southern counties have long demonstrated the northward movement of Hispanic Catholicism into Colorado. At the same time, however, the predominance of Methodist counties along the wholly Methodist Kansas border suggests the east-ward movement of that denomination. In 2000, the state had 18 counties that were predominantly Methodist and four in which Presbyterians were the majority. In two counties, Lutherans were in the majority, and this was also true of four other Protestant counties, one each for the Episcopalians, the Congregationalists (UCC), Baptists (all varieties), and the Disciples of Christ. Twenty-eight counties were predominantly Catholic.[16] Colorado's more complex patterns and larger population reflect its history: ongoing Hispanic settlement from the south, the Santa Fe trade from the east, the north-south railway connection linking Cheyenne and northern New Mexico, mining rushes across the region, agricultural settlement, Mexican immigration, and so on.

Like Montana and Colorado, Wyoming too reflected historical settlement pat-terns, though these were somewhat simpler in nature. Wyoming populations clus-tered around the major east-west and north-south corridors (essentially, the Overland Trail/Union Pacific route and the Bozeman Trail), and the rest of the state remained relatively sparsely settled. One good missionary might be enough to win over such thinly populated Wyoming counties as Sublette or Niobrara (both Congregationalist), or Crook, Converse, or Washakie (all Methodist). Not surpris-ingly, the railroad towns tended to be largely Catholic, while the Utah and Idaho border areas have always been influenced by nearby Mormon settlements.

By the 1990s, a number of changes were visible across the northern Rockies, the complex result of shifting populations and transformations in church practice. Catholic-predominated counties grew steadily in Colorado, from 28 in 1952 to 42 in 1971 to 50 in 1990. Much of that shift came at the expense of older mainline Protestantism—Episcopalians, Presbyterians, and especially Methodists—and it suggests the significant demographic role of Latino/a immigration and labor, as well as an upsurge in conservative Protestantism. In addition, Mormon missions had created pockets of strength across the area. In Wyoming, for example, no counties were predominantly Mormon in 1971; by 1990, six were.

In Colorado, by 2000 one could find two different patterns. Along the eastern borders of Colorado and New Mexico ran a set of contiguous counties in which evangelical Protestant adherents made up at least 15 percent of the total popula-tion, suggesting a general movement of southern evangelicalism across the thresh-old into the region. At the same time, a diverse set of evangelical counties spread across Colorado, Wyoming, and Montana (including Colorado Springs' El Paso county) suggesting the beginnings and even flourishing of a regional evangelical culture in the northern Rockies.

In all three states, year 2000 surveys suggested that evangelical Protestants made up roughly two thirds of all Protestant congregations, and from 11 percent (Colorado) to 12 percent (Wyoming) of the total state populations. Given the relatively greater density of Colorado (which had roughly 4.3 million people in comparison to Wyoming's 493,000 and Montana's 902,000), the number of people claiming evangelical beliefs in Colorado have come to represent a significant political power base. If the number of evangelical and other conservative Christian congregations in all the three states are considered, it becomes clear that Colorado's western slope and eastern plains counties are clearly the most conservative religious areas in the sub-region.

In general, however, new kinds of enclaves seem to be forming in the area. Growing Catholic clusters are likely to be defined in terms of ethnicity, while the increase in many evangelical and conservative enclaves can often be most easily visible in terms of the political ideologies that accompany particular expressions of faith. In a few cases, class-based religious enclaves have also become visible. In general, the concentrations of wealth gathered around ski areas and vacation retreats such as Aspen, Vail, Jackson Hole, Big Sky, and others have remained largely secular. But in places such as Crestone, Colorado, one can find economic elites with connections to global markets and capital retreating to the hills to find a particularly spiritual peace. Living in gated retirement subdivisions (not far from San Luis), residents are close to Zen and Tibetan Buddhist retreats, a Hindu Ashram, and a Carmelite monastery, not to mention New Age simulations, given shape in monuments like "Cresthenge" (a model of Stonehenge), a labyrinth that mimics the one at Chartres Cathedral, and even a reproduction of a ziggurat.[17]

But, as we have seen, the region's religious expressions are not always so diverse, global, and cosmopolitan. In 1992, Colorado became the first state to pass an amendment prohibiting localities from outlawing discrimination against homosexuals. Seeking to proclaim Colorado Springs "the Vatican of evangelical Christians," voters there approved the measure by a 2:1 ratio and some leaders spoke openly about their desire to "liberate" the city from homosexuality, and to found it as a beachhead for similar liberations throughout the state and region. The amendment, which originated with the Colorado Springs-based group Colorado for Family Values, brought together El Paso county's evangelical social conservatism with the "rugged individualist" cultural conservatism of the state's eastern plains and western slope residents, suggesting the power that might be wielded by such an alliance. And indeed, the California fiscal conservative cum Colorado Springs resident, Douglas Bruce, was able to rally the evangelical community and the cultural/economic conservatives to his own particular cause, passing the 1992 Taxpayer's Bill of Rights (TABOR) amendment, which requires any tax increases to be put to statewide vote.

Colorado Springs' political culture mingled together these economic, political, social, and religious positions, and that culture reached out across the state and
nation. The 1992 anti-gay amendment, though never free of court challenges and
overturned as unconstitutional by the U.S. Supreme Court in 1995, spawned similar efforts at state and local levels in Maine, Oregon, Washington, and Ohio. Anti-
gay hate crimes such as the savage beating death of the gay college student
Matthew Shepherd in Laramie cannot be directly attributed to the mingling of
these conservatisms coming out of El Paso county, but it is not unreasonable to see
those conservatisms in the larger political climate of the northern Rockies/plains
region.

In 2000, evangelical voters in the Mountain West polled slightly above the
national average in their opposition to civil rights protections for gays and lesbians. The only group visibly against gay civil rights, 52.8 percent of western
evangelical voters opposed it. In line with other conservative positions, they tended in larger percentages to reject environmental protections, national health care,
and welfare support. Focus on the Family, not surprisingly, reacted with horror to
the 2003 Supreme Court decision *Lawrence v. Texas*, which found gay sexual practice protected by the right to privacy, and they followed the party line in horror-
mongering a whole wash of other soon-to-be licit activities, such as bestiality and
incest.

The reporting surrounding Matthew Shepherd's 1998 murder took on a distinctly religious cast; Shepherd, who was beaten, tied to a fence, and left to die,
was frequently represented in terms of crucifixion. The Shepherd attack did lead,
however, to a concentrated backlash against some of the activities of the Christian
political right. As Kim Mills of the Human Rights Committee observed following
Shepherd's murder:

> The leaders of the most powerful religious political organizations—
> some of which have headquarters right here in Colorado—have made
> strategic political decision to target gays and lesbians. These groups
> include Focus on the Family and its political offshoot, the Family
> Research Council; the Christian Coalition; Coral Ridge Ministries;
> and a host of others. Make no mistake; this campaign against gay
> people is not about religion or redemption or any of those other "spir-
> itual" terms they might use in their advertising or public relations.
> They are looking for wedge issues that will help them elect more
> staunch religious political conservatives at all levels of government.[18]

Though Shepherd's death, combined with the 1995 Oklahoma City bombing,
may have suppressed the rhetoric surrounding the fusion of anti-government and

social conservatism in the northern Rockies, it remains a powerful political force with substantive ambitions.

In 1996, Focus on the Family's James Dobson told his 5 million weekly listeners that he would not vote for Robert Dole because the Republican Party was "betraying" conservative evangelical voters. He threatened that such voters would either dominate the party or leave it behind. By 2000, with President George W. Bush's appointment of the conservative Christian ideologue John Ashcroft as Attorney General and numerous other appointments, it was clear that conservative evangelicals had in fact found a home in the party. If they did not completely dominate it (one might point here to pragmatic and largely secular geopolitical and economic conservativisms), they were able to require Republican obeisance on a number of issues.

Conclusion

An evangelical Christian sitting in Colorado Springs in 2003 might be tempted to sigh and view the northern plains and mountains states as largely unfinished business. Catholicism was growing across the region as the Latino/a demographic sector increased in population number and percentage. Mormonism had made inroads in the areas surrounding Utah, particularly in Wyoming; and Methodists (in Colorado) and Lutherans (in Montana) retained much of their historical strength. Meanwhile, Boulder's cosmopolitan New Age practices had been reproduced in Crestone, which had set itself up as a wealthy enclave of dabblers in Buddhism and other exotic traditions.

And if Wyoming and Montana had nothing to compare with Boulder, Crestone, Santa Fe, or Sedona, both states had lingering pockets of New Age and alternative religious practice, typically attached to university communities such as Bozeman, Helena, and Laramie. Native American reservations continued to function as religious enclaves in their own right, complex, but with a growing focus on the reclamation and practice of traditional religion. And, of course, the bottom line was that, across the region, more than half the population remained unchurched.

But a Boulder Unitarian might be as inclined to survey the same terrain and feel a trifle beleaguered, as if an emerging religious and political clarity was threatening the cosmopolitan openness of the area. Colorado, which had tended through much of the last 50 years to balance its congressional politics between Democrats and Republicans, had in 2003 two Republican senators. Five of its seven congressional districts were held by Republicans (only the districts encompassing Boulder and Denver's working class and African-American neighborhoods were Democratic), as were the governorship and the state legislature. Those political realities—and the kinds of social, economic, and environmental positions they reflected—seemed to suggest that evangelical organizations like Focus on the Family had succeeded in imprinting their beliefs on the political process.

The seeming clarity was not only political. Our Boulder resident might also worry that the region was losing its religious diversity, as it was populated by increasing numbers of people loyal to the Catholic Church. Likewise, in addition to the imported, organization-based fundamentalism characteristic of Colorado Springs, the three states were all becoming home to increasing numbers of adherents to powerful southern evangelical traditions. In each state, more than half of the Protestant population saw itself as evangelical (in Colorado, 61.6 percent; in Wyoming, 56.8 percent; and in Montana, 51.7 percent). It certainly might seem that the historical diversity of the northern Rockies and Plains was on the verge of giving way to a new religious clarity, as the sub-region threatened to become predominantly Catholic and evangelical, with some small areas remaining Mormon, Lutheran, Methodist, or "other."

The political pendulum, for the moment, seems to have swung in favor of the ambitions of the religious right. A number of legislative initiatives—prisons and highways over education; resource development over conservation and preservation; conservative social programs—make this clear. A brief perusal of the Web sites of the region's Republican representatives suggests how attuned those lawmakers are to the social and political agenda of the religious right. One might argue, however, that it would be a mistake to overestimate the power behind that agenda, at least in Colorado, Wyoming, and Montana. In these states, religious conservatism lives in powerful relation to other forms of conservatisms. In Montana and Wyoming (and to a lesser degree, Colorado), the mindset surrounding extractive economies continues to drive political conservatism in critical ways. And social conservatisms have traditionally been contested in these states, with large-scale impulses toward social conformity clashing with the desires of groups and individuals to live according to their own beliefs. In Colorado Springs, for example, the passage of the anti-gay amendment helped create a visible enclave of gay rebellion within the city itself.

Even in relation to the rest of the Mountain West states, Colorado, Wyoming, and Montana seem comparably less driven by the evangelical agenda (although it should be noted that for political purposes, this agenda is often quietly masked and "secularized" for popular consumption). The sub-region has, compared to Arizona, New Mexico, Idaho, and Utah, the *lowest* percentages of evangelical Protestants and/or Mormons. And, as noted before, as long as the level of the unchurched, the "Nones," remains at more than half, just how much cultural and political power religion will be able to exert in the region remains an open question. Perhaps the answer emanating from both Boulder and Colorado Springs is this: religion will always structure the exercise of political, social, economic, and legal power in important ways. But, as with most things, religious cultural politics will be constantly contested, both from within and without. The Christian Right's purchase on the region will never be as secure as some in the Springs would desire, nor as dominating as some in Boulder might fear. Demography, immigration, schisms, and outright opposition will, as with any social formation, check ambitions and transform religious practices in complex ways. In that reality, perhaps the states of the northern Rockies and Plains hold a lesson for us all.

Endnotes

1. See, for example, Laura Wilson, *Hutterites of Montana* (New Haven: Yale University Press, 2000).
2. www.buddhanet.net/americas/usa_co.html
3. The numbers of nuns in the cloister grew so much that, in 1989, St. Walburga achieved abbey status. By 1992, it became clear that the nuns needed both more workspace and larger living quarters in order to continue to accept new members. According to their own history (posted at http://www.walburga.org/Archives.html), they considered various options for expansion. "We realized that our Boulder location, by this time on a busy highway and surrounded by subdivisions, was not the right place to build a new monastery. So, in 1997, after five years of planning, discussion, and preparation, our community relocated to our present site in Virginia Dale, Colorado, on land donated to us by a generous Denver businessman and his wife."
4. In 1922, this congregation united with St. Stephen's Episcopal Church and together they built a church whose tower is a copy of the tower of Magdalen College, Oxford University, England. Its Web site indicates that the Anglican connection is kept alive today: "the magnificent stained glass windows, splendid reredos and excellent music enhance the traditional Anglican worship of Grace Church and St. Stephen's Parish" http://www.graceandststephens.org/history.html.
5. For Focus, see www.family.org.
6. For Minnery, see "Focus on the Family Official Challenges Christians to Influence Politics, Culture." www.family.org/welcom/press/a0020760.cfm.
7. See, for an explicit treatment of Indian hymn singing, Luke Eric Lassiter, Clyde Ellis, and Ralph Kotay, *The Jesus Road: Kiowas, Christianity, and Indian Hymns* (Lincoln: University of Nebraska Press, 2002).
8. For a powerful treatment of the significance of place, in an Apache context, see Keith Basso, *Wisdom Sits in Places: Landscape and Language Among the Western Apache* (Albuquerque: University of New Mexico Press, 1996).

9. On Devil's Tower, see Wendy Rex-Atzet, "Narratives of Place and Power: Laying Claim to Devil's Tower," in *Imagining the Big Open: Nature, Identity, and Play in the New West.* Ed. (Elaine Bapis, Thomas Harvey, and Liza Nicholas) (Salt Lake City: University of Utah Press, 2002).

10. For a richer discussion, see John Wunder, *Retained by the People: A History of American Indians and the Bill of Rights* (New York: Oxford, 1994); 193-198. See also Suzan Shown Harjo, "American Indian Religious Freedom Act at 25," *Indian Country Today* (August 1, 2003),. http://www.indian-country.com/article/1059748335.

11. See David Hurst Thomas, *Skull Wars: Kennewick Man, Archaeology, and the Battle for Native American Identity* (New York: Basic, 2000).

12. Ferenc Morton Szasz, *The Protestant Clergy in the Great Plains and Mountain West, 1865-1915* (Albuquerque: University of New Mexico Press, 1988): 177-178.

13. Frederick E. Hoxie, *Parading Through History: The Making of the Crow Nation in America 1805-1935* (Cambridge: Cambridge University Press, 1995): 197-225.

14. E.P. Tenney, *The New West as Related to the Christian College* (as quoted in Szasz, 18).

15. www.sanluiscolorado.org/shrine.html

16. Glenmary Survey, 1952. Denominational Rank by County.

17. http://www.crestonevisit.com/03/pages/06.html. I would also like to acknowledge the ongoing dissertation work of Tracy Brady, a Ph.D. candidate at the University of Colorado, who is currently working on Crestone's religious communities.

18. "Human Rights Campaign condemns Wyoming hate crime and says religious rights anti-gay rhetoric creates an atmosphere conducive to Violence", Press release, Saturday, October 10, 1998. http://uwacadweb.uwyo.edu/lgbta/mat-tnews.htm.

CHAPTER SIX

CONCLUSION:
SACRED LANDSCAPES IN TRANSITION

Jan Shipps

R egions in the continental United States are bounded spaces in which states with contiguous borders are situated in shared geographical areas. In addition to place, the various regions ordinarily have common histories in which newcomers with roughly comparable backgrounds and/or reasons for leaving where they once lived shared enough experiences to create distinctive cultures. The Mountain West is a conspicuous exception to this pattern. Its history does not unite; it divides. About the only dimensions of past experience this area's settlers had in common were those shared with all the other original European-American settlers—the necessity of dealing with native populations and the travails of pioneer lives.

This absence of a region-wide shared history lends power to the notion that geography was, and to a considerable extent continues to be, the principal agent of what might be described as region construction. Surely, from the perspective of religion, it is the landscape more than anything else that creates a regional consciousness. This appears to be true even among the half of the total population (48.3 percent) who fit into the no religious affiliation, or "None," category.

The sheer magnificence of the lofty heights of the Rockies, the Grand Tetons, and the Wasatch and Oquirrh mountain chains inspire awe. No affiliation with some religious organization is needed for the splendor of the grasslands of the high plains, the open ranges, the intermountain meadows, and the extraordinary color and terrible beauty of the deserts and canyon lands to generate evident veneration, although that reverence is often expressed through silence or with some much stronger variations of "Gee Whiz."

Helen Hunt Jackson, the champion of the rights of Native Americans, used Christian concepts to describe the "preternatural" beauty of what she could see from Colorado Springs, a harmony of mountains (including Pike's Peak) and plains where "the whole rounded horizon" is full of beauty and grandeur, to which is added "the subtle and indescribable spell of the rarefied air and light of 6,000 feet above the sea." It was in the east, she said, "that wise men saw the star. But it was westward to a high mountain, in a lonely place, that the disciples were led for the transfiguration."[1]

While more often stated in naturalistic or perhaps pantheistic terms, a sense of wonder that cannot be entirely obliterated by graffiti or other forms of human desecration is created when people wait patiently for the sunrise to illuminate Red Rocks, Denver's gorgeous natural amphitheater. Or when they listen to the absolute silence in Mesa Verde National Park, observe the Sea of Galilee-like vision of Bear Lake from the overlook that extends to the east above the Utah-Idaho border, or watch the sunset from the balcony outside El Tovar, the historic Fred Harvey eatery that sits 20 feet from the very edge of the south rim of the Grand Canyon. Indeed, the Mountain West's geographic wonders put humanity in its place by establishing just where men, women, boys, and girls fit in the grand scheme of things.

At a less impressionistic, more practical level, this area's geography mandates another regional commonality, the oasis-like character of community in the Mountain West. The North American Religion Atlas (NARA) data describing county congregational patterns reveal the outcome of this settlement pattern for organized religion. Although the Mountain West is lightly inhabited in per-square-mile terms, that habitation is not spread equally across the region. As would be expected, densely populated areas have congregations of substantial size, while rural areas have small, almost isolated, congregations. But size is not the only difference; there is considerable variation in the amount of religious diversity across the region, even outside Utah and southern Idaho.

Again, as expected, large churches built and maintained by congregations of surprising size exist in the region's cities and suburbs, while in the many counties where per-square-mile population is practically low enough to make them frontier-like places, congregations struggle to keep body and soul together. Quite naturally, urban and suburban situations allow organizational groupings of all sorts (Catholics, all kinds of Protestants, Latter-day Saints, Jews, and even "others"). But religious diversity is minimal or practically non-existent in tiny towns, villages, and hamlets.

This, as Kathleen Flake has shown, is surely the case in Mormon country. To a lesser extent, however, this is the pattern throughout the region. In western Colorado and Wyoming, northern Arizona and New Mexico, where Latter-day Saints are settling into all the areas that the early adherents to the faith claimed as the "State of Deseret," the lone congregation is often Mormon. Elsewhere, lightly populated settlements tend to have one Catholic and, at most, two small struggling Protestant congregations—one evangelical and the other a congregation of one of the historic mainline Protestant denominations. This isolated congregational configuration has made it possible—as Randi Walker's description of the recent scandals in New Mexico indicates—for Catholic bishops to quietly assign priests with records of sexual abuse to remote Catholic congregations (perhaps most especially Native American parishes). But sexual abuse is neither simply a Catholic nor a rural problem. A Protestant doctor cum evangelical congregational leader in Lovell, Wyoming, was convicted of multiple counts of molestation and rape.[2] Protestant clergy have also been accused of sexual indiscretions—some variation of the preacher-choir director liaisons of popular story—but such problems are as likely to arise in urban and suburban congregations as in rural ones. In Protestant denominations, accused ministers are rarely, if ever, reassigned to different congregations. The same is true when sexual abuse rears its ugly head in Mormonism. Several Mormon lay pastors (denominated bishops) have also been accused of sexual abuse.[3] Although the Mormon ward system is analogous to the Catholic parish system, the shifting of LDS lay pastors from one ward to another does not happen because bishops who preside over wards are called from within the wards themselves. Moreover, since disciplinary action occurs at the local level, repetition of this unhappy pattern is, at the very least, unlikely.

Despite its peculiar sub-regional configuration, another characteristic common all across the Mountain West is that the religious folk in the region are divided into two general types: people like Indians, Jews, Mormons, and to a certain extent Roman Catholics, whose religious identity is virtually a birthright; and others, generally Protestants, as well as those who say that they are "spiritual but not religious," whose religious identity is acquired rather than inborn. In the first instance—Mormons call this phenomenon being "born under the covenant;" Indians and Jews call it ethnicity—practice is not always the key to understanding where individuals fit within the regional religious array. Connections to traditions through parents, friends, and community may be more important than religious practice, making for individuals who are culturally but not religiously Indian, Jewish, Mormon, or Roman Catholic.[4] Among Protestants and "religious free lancers," membership and/or participation in ritualized activities, as well as assent to doctrinal positions, is more critical to religious identity.

A popular perception that relies on membership and adherent statistics holds that the Mountain West is, next to the Pacific Northwest, the most unchurched region in the nation. This perception may be mistaken because the groups whose identity is as often cultural or ethnic as it is religious—especially Catholics, Mormons, and Native Americans—are strong in this region, but they do not get counted as church adherents. The existence of an unspecified number of people who are culturally but not actively religious is an important element of religion's story in this region.

Clearly connected at a foundational level to this matter of how religious identity and ethnicity are related in exceedingly complex ways in this region is the fact that two of the Mountain West's sub-regions share another characteristic. Both the Arizona-New Mexico and the Utah-Idaho sub-regions have virtual establishments of religion. Until Arizona and New Mexico became U.S. territories in the mid-nineteenth century, Roman Catholicism was, quite literally, the established church, first as part of the Spanish Empire and then of the Mexican government. Even after these two territories became states, Roman Catholicism maintained its position as a quasi-establishment, leaving other religious organizations in these two states with the status of "tolerated" institutions.

Statistics are helpful, but they rarely tell the entire story. Making sense of how critical this quasi-establishmentarianism is to understanding religion in the southwestern sub-region of the Mountain West is revealed by comparing the place of Roman Catholicism in New England with its place in Arizona and New Mexico. The New England region has well over three times the percentage of Roman Catholics (68.5) in the total population as are reported for Arizona (19 percent) and almost twice the percentage reported for New Mexico (36.9). Yet the perception of Catholic hegemony seems to be much stronger in this part of the Mountain West than it is in New England.

A reasonable explanation for this is that, except for the indigenous population, Catholicism was not simply the legally established church in the Southwest. It was there first and claimed the ground and its inhabitants for Rome. In New England, Protestantism had been on the ground for more than a century before substantial numbers of Catholics arrived. Although the percentage of Catholics has overwhelmed the percentage of Protestants in the New England population for generations, the perception of whose land it is has never fully shifted from Protestants to Catholics.

In Utah and southern Idaho, the numbers almost tell the whole story. But not quite, especially for a place like metropolitan Salt Lake City where the population is almost evenly divided between Mormons and non-Mormons, with the latter a combination of Protestant, Catholic, Jewish, Islamic, and unchurched people apparently gaining in proportion to the active Latter-day Saint membership. There and elsewhere along the Mormon corridor, the fact that the Church of Jesus Christ of Latter-day Saints is virtually an established church is crucial to any deep comprehension of the story of this sub-region.

How the Church of Jesus Christ of Latter-day Saints maintains this position is revealed through close observation of the history of the Mormons in Utah from its beginnings to the present day. In point of fact, in the formative years of the Great Basin Kingdom (the area the government would insist on calling Utah territory), a theocracy existed in the Great Salt Lake Valley and its environs because presidential appointments had handed the civil government over to the church authorities.

For several years, church authorities were the civil authorities, and vice versa, but the outcome of the Utah-Mormon War in 1857 brought this official theocratic system to an end.

The key concept here is official. Governor Brigham Young maintained that, although a "Gentile" federal official occupied the territorial governor's chair, he would continue to govern until the Lord released him from that obligation.[5] Creating a shadow government for the so-called State of Deseret, the Mormons convened each day after the territorial legislature met to ratify the passage of statutes and approve or disapprove other legislative actions. This, however, was a temporary continuation of theocracy that gradually gave way to the virtual establishment that still exists.

All sorts of religious organizations other than the Church of Jesus Christ of Latter-day Saints are welcome in Mormon country. But LDS political and economic power operates to make them lesser lights. Sometimes, non-Mormon religious organizations gratefully accept financial assistance from the LDS Church in the maintenance of their historic religious structures—the Roman Catholic Cathedral is a case in point. And most are willing to allow the Saints to do the lion's share of faith-based social service.

Baptists, especially, complain about Mormon cultural dominance, endlessly arguing that Mormonism is not Christian. But their efforts to attract Latter-day Saints away from Mormonism are hampered by a reality of Mormon ethnicity that makes true conversion difficult. In interviews with this author, the bishops of several Salt Lake City Mormon wards estimated that about a third of the ward was made up of people who had been either Protestant or Catholic, while the ministers of several Protestant and one Catholic congregation also opined that about a third of their flocks were made up of people who used to be Mormon. But this circulation of the Saints—"Saints" in a generic sense, including Methodists, Baptists, Catholics, and so on, as well as Mormons—situation appears to be a surface phenomenon.

According to the Rev. Mike Gray, pastor of Southeastern Baptist Church, the largest Southern Baptist congregation in the Salt Lake valley since the 1980s, despite proselytizing in both directions, Protestants and Mormons share the same physical universe but more or less keep to themselves. In a statement that reveals how the establishment works in the culture, Pastor Gray adds that he is sending his college-age children out of the state for their educations. "If they go to college in Utah, the Mormons will probably get them," he said.

Despite several significant exceptions—the work of Patricia Limerick, Walter Nugent, and Dean May in particular—histories of the Mountain West and histories of the American West in general are strangely revealing of the general religious situation in this region. Non-Mormon historians have, in the words of the eminent his-

torian Richard White, "more or less decided to skip Utah." They write the story of
the states all around the Mormon corridor, leaving the middle empty, almost as if it
did not exist. A pastry metaphor sums things up; they write Western history as if it
were a doughnut, leaving historians of the Latter-day Saints to fill in the hole.

While cultural integration proceeded as Mormon politicians and financiers
became familiar public figures, until the last two or three decades of the twentieth
century the historiography of the American West reflected the isolation of
Mormonism from the remainder of American religion. Long regarded as vaguely
foreign and surely heretical (especially when plural marriage was an acceptable
form of marriage within the Mormon faith), the religion started to shed its nineteenth-century stereotype during the Great Depression when the *Reader's Digest*,
the *Saturday Evening Post*, and other periodicals pointed to the way "the Mormons
take care of their own." Their abstinence from alcohol, tobacco, and coffee, and
their potent patriotism were also often mentioned in the media. And the 1950s
drumbeat for "having faith in faith" made the commitment of Latter-day Saints to
their church so admirable that a group that was once denigrated and outcast became
one that was admired. But unlike Catholicism and Judaism, Mormonism was never
integrated into the nation's religious culture. Yet that may be occurring as this
account of Religion in the Mountain West is being prepared. Although more Latter-
day Saints live outside than inside the United States, the Church of Jesus Christ of
Latter-day Saints is now the sixth largest religious institution in the nation. The
answer to the question, "Where are the Mormons" was once, Utah (and Southern
California and the rest of the Mountain West). But increasingly, the proper answer
is "everywhere."

In the Mountain West, however, the extension of Mormonism is both a religious and a geographic story. In 1852, when the Mormons first petitioned the government for statehood, they presented a map of the State of Deseret that included
all of Utah, southern Idaho, western Wyoming and Colorado, northern Arizona and
New Mexico, as well as a corridor to southern California that would provide access
to a Pacific seaport. Congress not only said no to statehood, but it reduced the
boundaries of Utah Territory essentially to the current boundaries of the state.
NARA data examined at the county level indicate that what is now happening is
that Saints are filling in the boundaries of the State of Deseret. The pastry metaphor
will soon be less useful, for the hole in the doughnut is gradually expanding so
much that the metaphor does not increase understanding of the Mountain West. As
the chapters in this book make clear, religion in this region is not as static as it was
even two or three decades ago. The areas around Phoenix and Tucson are taking on
the character of Los Angeles, as (I am told) is St. George, Utah. New Mexico is
becoming more rather than less Catholic. The percentage of Catholics in the
Montana population is also escalating, but a new LDS temple in Billings, Montana,

is evidence that an increasing number of Latter-day Saints are residing outside the traditional boundaries of the State of Deseret. And the existence of a traditionally neutral or at least religiously undefined arena in Colorado and Wyoming could be turning into an evangelical stronghold.

Although the importance of the landscape as the truly defining feature of religion in this region will not be overshadowed by these shifts in religious demography, they are critical to the story of the modern Mountain West because they help to push religion out of the private into the public sphere. In the sub-regions of the Mountain West that have quasi-establishments, religion's role in public life and the creation of distinctive cultures has never been hidden. But especially in Colorado, Wyoming, Montana, and northern Idaho (the Rocky Mountain states), this public dimension of what, for so long, was relegated to the private sphere is newly apparent in the life of the Mountain West.

Certainly religion appears to be having an impact on the political life of the region. The shift of the solid South from Democrat to Republican usually headlines stories about the alteration in the national political environment that occurred in the second half of the twentieth century. There the impetus was race. Here religion may be more of a stimulus for a change that is not as often noticed, but is surely as real.

Conservatism as it is expressed in the Republican Party has arguably become the political establishment in the Mountain West. Yet rather than the formation of a solid block of Republican states in the familiar solid South pattern, what seems to be transpiring in this region is the materializing of a striated conservative block shot through with furrows and ridges of liberalism that reflects the environmentalist temper of the region, with a frontier mentality of the old west with its openness to experimentation and change, and with a libertarian state of mind—in all of which religion is imbedded enough to be influential.

A good way to track the emergence of this trend is through an examination of the region's election returns. Over the last two decades of the twentieth century, the outcome of the federal election races for president and vice-president and for Congress has increased Republican hegemony. With the exception of Arizona, every state in the region voted for Lyndon Johnson in the 1964 presidential election. But in all the national elections between 1968 and 1988 every state in the region—even New Mexico—voted Republican. During the 1990s that solidity gave way. Colorado, Montana, and New Mexico voted for Bill Clinton in 1992, but Colorado and Montana returned to the Republican fold in 1996 while Arizona joined New Mexico in voting to re-elect Clinton. In 2000, only New Mexico voted for Al Gore.

In elections for the House of Representatives and the Senate, the regional shift toward the Republicans was even more apparent. In 1993, almost half (48 percent) of the Congressmen from the Mountain West in the House of Representatives were

Democrats. By 2001, that percentage had fallen to 14.3. Representation in the Senate has been slightly more balanced; since 1993 two of the region's states (Montana and New Mexico) have had one Democratic and one Republican senator. Since 1997, however, both senators from all five of the other states have been Republican.

Where the trend toward conservatism is even more evident is in the state legislatures and governorships. In every state except New Mexico, almost two-thirds of the legislators in the lower houses have been Republican.[6] The proportion of Republican legislators in the upper houses is not quite so high. But the average in the past four elections has been above 60 percent. Even in traditionally Democratic New Mexico, the percentage was up to 56 percent in 2000, though it dipped to 50 percent in Arizona and 49 percent in Colorado. In 1990, four of the seven states in the region had governors who were Democrats. In 2000, only two of the states (Arizona and New Mexico) had Democratic governors.

Establishing a direct correlation between the trend toward political conservatism and the shifting religious mosaic in the Mountain West is not possible. But the American Religious Identification Survey (ARIS) data for the region reveal that the people who identify themselves with specific religious denominations, churches, or traditions are more likely to register to vote (78 percent) than those who say they have no "religion" or refuse to answer (67 percent). Moreover, the weighted percentages provided by analysts of the ARIS data reveal a surprisingly consistent pattern of more Republicans than Democrats.

As might be anticipated, the party preference of both Catholic and Protestant Hispanic voters is heavily Democratic, but among virtually all the others with specific religious identifications there are more voters with Republican than Democratic Party affiliations. The percentage is more than twice as high for white, non-Hispanic Catholics (42 percent as opposed to 20 percent); for white evangelical Protestants the proportion is even less balanced (56 percent as opposed to 15 percent); and for Mormons the Republican-Democratic proportions are 58 percent to 17 percent.

Perhaps accounting for the striations in the Republican block are fairly high percentages of independents: 33 percent for white non-Hispanic Catholics and 39 for Hispanic Catholics; and an average of 28 percent for white mainline Protestants, white evangelical and unspecified Protestant Christians. But party affiliation, or lack of it, may well be less important than the western temperament, as revealed in the career and actions of such a quintessentially Mountain Western figure as Sandra Day O'Connor. She is an Episcopalian U.S. Supreme Court justice whose profound conservatism has limits that reach far beyond the region to affect the entire nation.

The Bliss Institute's National Surveys of Religion and Politics across the decade of the 1990s are also revealing. Compared with national data, data for the

Mountain West show that evangelicals with high commitment to the faith are slightly more liberal than is true elsewhere in the U.S.; those with low commitment are considerably less liberal but far more independent. In the Mountain West, historic mainline Protestants—whether with high or low commitment—are more conservative than their fellows in the rest of the nation. Whatever their level of commitment, Catholics in the region are also more conservative than Catholics throughout the United States. And Latter-day Saints (along with the Eastern Orthodox, black Catholics, and others in the "other Christian" category in the Mountain West) are far more conservative than are the members of these groups in the rest of the nation.

On specific issues there is considerable difference among the adherents of the various groups within the region. With regard to views about whether abortion should be legal, almost twice as many evangelicals with high commitment are conservative than are evangelicals with low commitment. Catholics with high commitment are almost as conservative as evangelicals with high commitment, but Catholics with low commitment are considerably less conservative than evangelicals with low commitment. Attitudes about gay rights are almost the same, more liberal than conservative, except in the case of those who fit into the category that includes Latter-day Saints. In that group, almost equal numbers were pro-gay rights and anti-gay rights, with a considerable group holding a moderate position standing in between.

Except for those who fit into the non-Christian category, none of the people in the Mountain West who fit into the religious categories are more liberal on the environment than is the case in the rest of the country. Perhaps this is explained by the fact that the liberal position was stated as one holding that "strict rules to protect the environment are necessary even if they cost jobs," a more idealistic and much more acceptable position in areas where the connection between the environment and human livelihoods is not so direct.

As interesting and useful as are the results of surveys and censuses, precise measurement of attitudes is as impossible as the precise measurement of religious adherence and religious commitment. Collections of data only point to the shape that reality takes, and as reality is ever-changing, data are forever revealing the way things were rather than the current state of existence on the ground. As such data often turn out to be poor predictors of what will happen next, how the story of religion in the Mountain West is likely to develop in the future is uncertain.

But the physical landscape is unlikely to change, which means that two things are reasonably certain. The landscape will continue to shape and influence both the private and public expression of religion in this region. Moreover, how and for whom the landscape is sacred is likely to remain in tension if not until the end of time, then at least for the foreseeable time to come.

Endnotes

1. *Westward to a High Mountain: The Colorado Writings of Helen Hunt Jackson*, ed. by Mark I. West (Denver: Colorado Historical Society, 1994), 20.
2. Jack Olsen, *"Doc": The Rape Of The Town Of Lovell* (New York: Atheneum, 1989).
3. Anson Shupe, *The Darker Side of Virtue: Corruption, Scandal, and the Mormon Empire* (New York: Prometheus Books, 1991), 113-115.
4. The problem of identifying where Native Americans fit in the religious pictures of particular areas is complicated by the fact that census data identify Indians as members of an ethnic group rather than as members of religious bodies while data gathered for the religious atlas do not include Native American faith groups.
5. Almost any standard Utah history outlines the story of the Mormons in politics. See, in particular, Edward Leo Lyman, *Political Deliverance: The Mormon Quest for Utah Statehood* (Urbana: University of Illinois Press, 1986).
6. The Republican majority dipped to 58 percent in 2000.
7. This chart of the percentage of Republicans in the state legislatures is revealing of the conservative trend in politics in the Mountain West.

	Lower House 1994	Lower House 1996	Lower House 1998	Lower House 2000
Arizona	63	63	63	64
Colorado	63	63	63	61
Idaho	81	84	84	87
Montana	67	65	65	58
New Mexico	34	40	40	40
Utah	73	73	72	67
Wyoming	78	71	71	76
Average	66	66	65	64

	Upper House 1994	Upper House 1996	Upper House 1998	Upper House 2000
Arizona	63	60	60	50
Colorado	54	57	57	49
Idaho	77	86	86	91
Montana	62	68	66	62
New Mexico	36	40	40	56
Utah	66	69	69	69
Wyoming	67	70	70	67
Average	61	64	64	63

APPENDIX

In order to provide the best possible empirical basis for understanding the place of religion in each of the religions of the United States, the Religion by Region project contracted to obtain data from three sources: the North American Religion Atlas (NARA); the 2001 American Religious Identification Survey (ARIS); and the 1992, 1996, and 2000 National Surveys of Religion and Politics (NSRP).

NARA For the Project, the Polis Center of Indiana University-Purdue University at Indianapolis created an interactive Web site that made it possible to map general demographic and religious data at the national, regional, state-by-state, and county-by-county level. The demographic data were taken from the 2000 Census. The primary source for the religious data (congregations, members, and adherents) was the 2000 Religious Congregations and Membership Survey (RCMC) compiled by the Glenmary Research Center. Because a number of religious groups did not participate in the 2000 RCMS—including most historically African-American Protestant denominations—this dataset was supplemented with data from other sources *for adherents only*. The latter included projections from 1990 RCMC reports, ARIS, and several custom estimates. For a fuller methodological account, go to *http://www.religionatlas.org*.

ARIS The American Religious Identification Survey (ARIS 2001), carried out under the auspices of the Graduate Center of the City University of New York by Barry A. Kosmin, Egon Mayer, and Ariela Keysar, replicates the methodology of the National Survey of Religious Identification (NSRI 1990). As in 1990 the ARIS sample is based on a series of national random digit dialing (RDD) surveys, utilizing ICR, International Communication Research Group in Media, Pennsylvania, national telephone omnibus services. In all, 50,284 U.S. households were successfully interviewed. Within a household, an adult respondent was chosen using the "last birthday method" of random selection. One of the distinguishing features of both ARIS 2001 and NSRI 1990 is that respondents were asked to describe themselves in terms of religion with an open-ended question: "What is your religion, if any?[1]" ARIS 2001 enhanced the topics covered by adding questions concerning

religious beliefs and membership as well as religious switching and religious identification of spouses/partners. The ARIS findings have a high level of statistical
significance for most large religious groups and key geographical units, such as
states. ARIS 2001 detailed methodology can be found in the report on the
American Religious Identification Survey 2001at *www.gc.cuny.edu/studies/aris-
_index.htm.*

NSRP The National Surveys of Religion and Politics were conducted in 1992,
1996, and 2000 at the Bliss Center at the University of Akron under the direction
of John C. Green, supported by grants from the Pew Charitable Trusts.

Together, these three surveys include more than 14,000 cases. Eight items
were asked in all three surveys (partisanship, ideology, abortion, gay rights, help
for minorities, environmental protection, welfare spending, and national health
insurance). The responses on these items were pooled for all three years to produce enough cases for an analysis by region. These data must be viewed with
some caution because they represent opinion over an entire decade rather than at
one point in time. A more detailed account of how these data were compiled may
be obtained from the Bliss Institute.

Endnote

1. In the 1990 NSRI survey, the question wording was: "What is your religion?" In the 2001 ARIS survey, the phrase, "...if any" was added to the
   question. A subsequent validity check based on cross-samples of 3,000
   respondents carried out by ICR in 2002 found no statistical difference
   between the pattern of responses according to the two wordings.

BIBLIOGRAHPY

Alexander, Thomas G. *Utah: The Right Place*. Layton, UT: Gibbs Smith, 1995. 2nd Revised Edition, 2003.

Encyclopedia Americana. International Ed. s.v. "Mormons." [Prepared by Jan Shipps with the needs of journalists in mind, this entry is a succinct summary of the history and belief system of the Latter-day Saints.]

Ivakhiv, Adrian J. *Claiming Sacred Ground: Pilgrims and Politics at Glastonbury and Sedona.* Bloomington: Indiana University Press, 2001.

Loftin, John D. Religion and Hopi Life in the Twentieth Century. Bloomington: Indiana University Press, 1991

Mauss, Armand L. *The Angel and the Beehive: The Mormon Struggle with Assimilation.*Urbana: University of Illinois Press, 1994.

Noel, Thomas J. *Colorado Catholicism and the Archdiocese of Denver, 1857-1989*. Niwot: University Press of Colorado, 1989.

Nugent, Walter. *Into the West: The Story of Its People*. New York: Alfred A. Knopf, 1999.

Ostling, Richard N. and Joan K. *Mormon America: The Power and the Promise*. San Francisco: HarperCollins Publishers, 1999.

Quinn, D. Michael. "Religion in the American West." In *Under an Open Sky:*

Rethinking America's Western Past, ed. Willian Cronon et al. New York: Norton, 1992, 145-66.

Shipps, Jan. *Sojourner in the Promised Land: Forty Years Among the Mormons.* Urbana-Champagne: University of Illinois Press. 2000.

Small, Lawrence F. ed. *Religion in Montana: Pathways to the Present.* Helena: Falcon Press. 1992.

Smith, Duane A. *Rocky Mountain West: Colorado, Wyoming, and Montana, 1859-1915*. Albuquerque: University of New Mexico Press, 1992.

Szasz, Ferenc M. and Etulain, Richard. *Religion in Modern New Mexico.* Albuquerque: University of New Mexico Press, 1997.

Szasz, Ferenc M. *Religion in the Modern American West.* Tucson: University of Arizona Press, 2000.

INDEX

CONTRIBUTORS

Philip Deloria is associate professor, department of history and program in American culture, at the University of Michigan. He is the author of *Playing Indian* (1998) and *Indians in Unexpected Places* (forthcoming, 2004). He also co-edited *The Blackwell Companion to American Indian History.*

Kathleen Flake is assistant professor of American religion, Vanderbilt University Divinity School and graduate department of religion. A former litigation attorney for the U.S. Government, she is the author of *The Politics of American Religious Identity: The Seating of Senator Reed Smoot, Mormon Apostle* (2004) as well as a variety of articles on Mormonism.

Walter Nugent is the Andrew V. Tackes Emeritus Professor of History at the University of Notre Dame. He is the author of *Into the West: The Story of Its People* (1999), a work that was honored by the Western History Association as the Best Book in Western History published in 1999. Among his many other books are *Structures of American Social History* (1981) and *Crossings: Transatlantic Population Movements, 1870-1914* (1992).

Jan Shipps is professor emeritus of religious studies and history at Indiana University-Purdue University, Indianapolis. A non-Mormon specialist on Mormonism, her principal published works are *Mormonism: The Story of a New Religious Tradition* (1985) and *Sojourner in the Promised Land: Forty Years among the Mormons* (2000), which was designated by the Mormon History Association as the Best Book on Mormon History in the year it was published.

Mark Silk is associate professor of religion and public life at Trinity College, Hartford, Connecticut, and founding director of the Leonard E. Greenberg Center for the Study of Religion and Public Life at Trinity. A former newspaper reporter and member of the editorial board of the *Atlanta Journal-Constitution,* he is author of *Spiritual Politics: Religion and America Since World War II* (1998; 2nd edition forthcoming) and *Unsecular Media: Making News of Religion in America*

(1995). He is editor of *Religion in the News*, a magazine published by the Greenberg Center that examines how the news media handle religious subject matter.

Ferenc Morton Szasz, professor of history at the University of New Mexico, is generally regarded as the leading authority on religion in the American West. Among his many publications are *The Divided Mind of Protestant America, 1880-1930* (1982); *The Protestant Clergy in the Great Plains and Mountain West, 1865-1915* (1988); and *Religion in the West* (2000).

Randi Jones Walker is associate professor of church history at Pacific School of Religion. She is the author of *Protestantism in the Sangre de Cristos 1850-1920* (1991), and *Emma Newman: A Frontier Woman Minister* (2000). Her *Evolution of a UCC Style: Essays in the History, Ecclesiology and Culture of the United Church of Christ* is forthcoming in 2004.